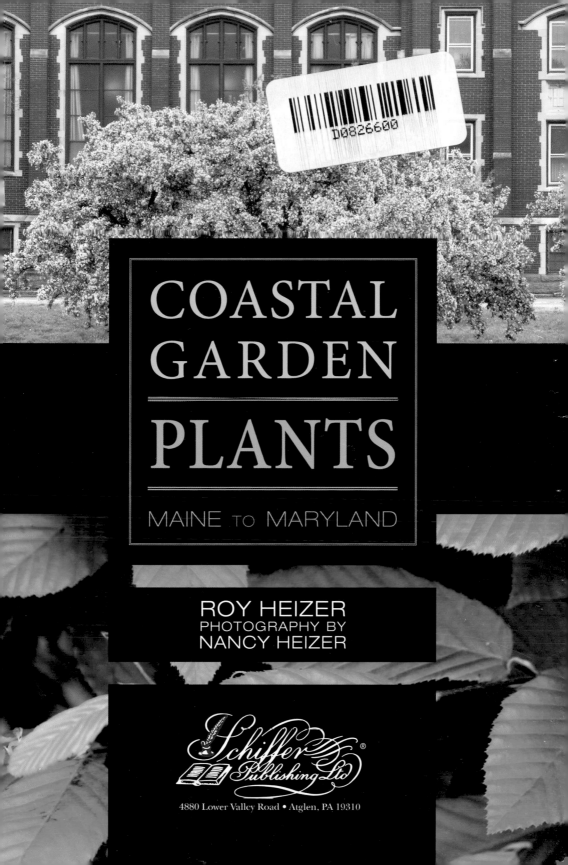

COASTAL GARDEN PLANTS

MAINE TO MARYLAND

ROY HEIZER
PHOTOGRAPHY BY
NANCY HEIZER

Schiffer
Publishing Ltd

4880 Lower Valley Road • Atglen, PA 19310

Other Schiffer Books by the Author:
Coastal Garden Plants: Florida to Virginia, ISBN: 978-0-7643-4181-6 $24.99
Atlanta's Garden Plants, ISBN: 978-0-7643-3810-6 $14.99
Savannah's Garden Plants, ISBN: 978-0-7643-3265-4 $9.99
Savannah's Historic Churches, ISBN: 978-0-7643-3864-9 $16.99

Designed by Justin Watkinson

Type set in Minion Pro/Zurich BT

ISBN: 978-0-7643-4402-2

Printed in China

Published by Schiffer Publishing, Ltd.
4880 Lower Valley Road
Atglen, PA 19310
Phone: (610) 593-1777; Fax: (610) 593-2002
E-mail: Info@schifferbooks.com

For the largest selection of fine reference books on this and related subjects, please visit our website at **www.schifferbooks.com**. You may also write for a free catalog.

This book may be purchased from the publisher.
Please try your bookstore first.

We are always looking for people to write books on new and related subjects. If you have an idea for a book, please contact us at
proposals@schifferbooks.com

Schiffer Books are available at special discounts for bulk purchases for sales promotions or premiums. Special editions, including personalized covers, corporate imprints, and excerpts can be created in large quantities for special needs. For more information contact the publisher.

In Europe, Schiffer books are distributed by
Bushwood Books
6 Marksbury Ave.
Kew Gardens
Surrey TW9 4JF England
Phone: 44 (0) 20 8392 8585; Fax: 44 (0) 20 8392 9876
E-mail: info@bushwoodbooks.co.uk
Website: www.bushwoodbooks.co.uk

T his book is dedicated to the many volunteers who work countless hours in America's community and botanical gardens. Your work has brought beauty, community, food and joy to the world…and it's a better place because of you! A special thank you to Michelle Obama, for inspiring our children to garden.

DEDICATION
ACKNOWLEDGMENTS

I'd like to thank my friends and family for their support of this project, and everyone at Schiffer Publishing. I would also like to thank the people of:
 Atlantic Canada
 Cape Cod, Massachusetts
 Coastal Connecticut
 Coastal Maine
 Delaware
 Long Island, New York
 New Jersey
 Rhode Island
 The Berkeley Community Garden,
  South Boston, Massachusetts
 The South Church Unitarian Universalist
  congregation in Portsmouth, New Hampshire

and the cities and towns of:
 Annapolis, Maryland
 Baltimore, Maryland
 Boston, Massachusetts
 Dover, Delaware
 Our Nation's Capital, Washington, D.C.
 Philadelphia, Pennsylvania
 Portsmouth, New Hampshire
 Salem, Massachusetts

A special thank you goes to New York City; your community gardens and innovative use of green space have been real inspirations.

CONTENTS

INTRODUCTION

The northern coastal region of the United States has an abundance of flowers, plants, and trees waiting to be explored by gardeners from all over the world. With this book as your guide, explore the folklore, history, and science of America's *Coastal Garden Plants: Maine to Maryland*. From New England to the Mid-Atlantic, gardeners will find fun facts and growing tips covering a wide range of ornamental plants and trees, as well as culinary and medicinal herbs.

What tree is a symbol of hope in the British Isles? Find out which garden plant helped a village survive an attack from a sea monster. Who is Francis Bacon, and what is his favorite herb? Can you name the fruiting tree that inspired a classic folk song? Appreciate which plants are thought to be sacred in various religious traditions and which are associated with ancient cultures.

The plants listed in this book are arranged in alphabetical order by botanical name, with an index of common names cross referenced for easy use. Featuring 120 plants and 420 full color digital photographs taken in their natural settings, this book makes plant identification quick and easy.

This book shares gardening suggestions and original tales about the annuals, perennials, shrubs, and trees along the coastal areas of Maine, New Hampshire, Massachusetts, Rhode Island, Connecticut, New York, New Jersey, Delaware, and Maryland. Read on and watch America's coastal plants blossom in your imagination!

COMMUNITY & PUBLIC GARDENS

Community Gardens, Greenways, and Public Greenspaces

No place in the United States is as crowded as the northeastern seaboard, with more people per square mile than anywhere else in America. Several of this country's largest cities are located near the coast between Maine and Maryland, and space physically to garden or just enjoy greenspace is becoming a premium. In these larger urban areas, Community and Public Gardens are sprouting up so that people can share natural beauty in the context of a city environment. Community and Public Gardens benefit a city by developing a sense of neighborhood through reducing crime and increasing positive local involvement. They decrease noise and chemical pollution, and provide markets and charities with a source of locally grown produce. Studies have shown that gardening and spending time in natural areas profoundly reduce stress, an important issue to those living in crowded urban centers.

While developers argue that greenspaces are unnecessary and take up valuable development space, the benefits of a community garden to the individual neighborhoods and the larger city are self-evident. Gardeners from Boston to Baltimore are extolling the virtues of community gardens, and more and more "extra" space within city limits are being taken over and converted to growing plots.

Municipal governments are even starting to realize the benefits of Community and Public Gardens in the form of city beautification. City managers and representatives appreciate that beautiful natural cityscapes draw

The Berkley Community Garden in Boston Massachusetts.

Community Garden

downtown residents, tourists, and corporate executives. Greenways and Greenspaces provide safe, traffic free areas for bicyclists, walkers, and events. Public Gardens attract people who, in turn, support downtown businesses and add to a cities sense of history.

Boston Common, the oldest public park in America, was established in 1634 to provide Boston residents a communal area. The Boston Public Garden, near Boston Common, was opened in 1837 as a public greenspace. It contains many mature trees and shrubs including Azaleas, Elms, Larches, Lindens, Oaks, Viburnums, Willows and Yews. The Boston Common and Boston Public Garden, as well as the Rose Fitzgerald Kennedy Greenway and Berkeley Community Gardens, add tremendously to the historical nature of Boston, providing locals and visitors alike large flower beds that display a wide range of flowers, shrubs, and trees.

In New York City, Central Park was first opened to the public in 1857. A year later, in 1858, it was expanded, utilizing a landscape design plan by Frederic Law Olmsted, widely considered America's first landscape architect, and his partner, Calvert Vaux. Central Park is a lushly landscaped greenspace in the heart of America's biggest city. Several large and small community gardens provide planting and display space to residents of New York's four other boroughs.

The public greenspaces listed here are just a few of the many Community and Public Gardens throughout the northeast; readers are encouraged to visit, appreciate and participate in all of them.

COMMUNITY GARDEN 3
Community Garden in Augusta, Maine.

COMMUNITY GARDEN 4
Community Garden

COMMUNITY GARDEN 5
Boston Public Gardens.

THE
PLANTS

Actinidia Kolomikta
Kolomikta Kiwi or Kiwi

A scandent woody vine, most American gardeners know this plant for its Kiwifruit, but it is also an ornamental vine for the northeastern garden.

Kolomikta Kiwi is a cold-hardy ornamental vine native to eastern Russia, China, and Japan. A scandent woody vine, Kolomikta Kiwi has heavily textured leaves that can occasionally display, even in the wild, the rare trait of white or pink variegation. A profusion of small, white and pinkish flowers are borne in mid-spring along the length of the vine. The flowers last for several weeks and are pollinated by beneficial insects in late spring and early summer. A dioecious perennial, Kolomikta Kiwi needs both a male and female specimen for successful fruit production. The pollinated flower then develops into a small Kiwi-like berry by late summer, providing a stunning fall display.

A deciduous vine, Kolomikta Kiwi showcases a wide range of fall color hues in the late season garden. Over the winter, Kolomikta Kiwi displays its rough bark and sprawling branches to great effect. Reliable to minus 10 degrees above ground, Kolomikta Kiwi returns each spring with vigor and on-going beauty.

A closely related species, Actinidia Deliciosa, produces the well-known, commercially significant, Kiwifruit. First cultivated in the late 19th century, Kiwifruit is a regularly consumed fruit in diets around the world.

A

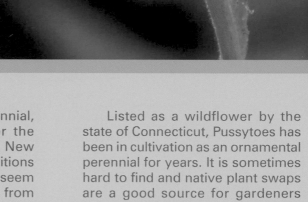

Pussytoes is a fun and reliable perennial most often planted for its woolly, silver-colored foliage.

A small, cold-hardy perennial, Pussytoes is well suited for the rocky shores of Maine and New Hampshire. The adverse conditions of the New England coastline seem unable to dissuade Pussytoes from thriving in colonies in and around dry, windswept, rocky out-croppings. Whirled rosettes of fleshy, silvery green leaves grow low to the ground, while the inflorescence peeks up no more than 6 inches to form mid-summer flowers. Both the leaves and the flower stalk of Pussytoes are softly pubescent, covered in a fine wooly texture. When the flowers of *Antennaria* open, the shape of the inflorescence resembles the outstretched paw of a kitten, hence the common name Pussytoes.

Listed as a wildflower by the state of Connecticut, Pussytoes has been in cultivation as an ornamental perennial for years. It is sometimes hard to find and native plant swaps are a good source for gardeners on the search for something fun. Pussytoes are hardy to Zone 3a.

Archeological excavations and archival records of colonial settlements in Maine have turned up evidence that *Antennaria* was utilized as early as 1725 along coastal areas. Thought to have magical powers over demons, it was used as part of exorcisms and other anti-witchcraft measures. *Antennaria*, in the form of dried leaves, were bundled along with other herbs to create ritualistic incenses.

Armeria

Thrift or Sea Thrift

Sea Thrift has white or reddish pink flowers in the summer months.

Grown in both American and English gardens, Sea Thrift has a long horticultural history.

While most kinds of Sea Thrift are native to the Mediterranean region of southern Europe, one type, *Armeria Maritima*, is native to the coastal areas of the British Isles. Sea Thrift was brought to America from Europe over two centuries ago, and it has naturalized in coastal areas of the northeast. A stylized depiction of the *Armeria Maritima* was featured on the reverse of the 1943 British Threepence coin. A collectable coin, this edition of the Threepence was produced in brass, making it rare among Threepence coins that are most often minted in silver. The Thrift's inclusion in British currency continues the long-standing tradition of floral symbology in municipal insignia.

Waving resolutely by the swirling sunny sea,
The Thrift it does seem mighty, against the raging breeze.
Graceful fists of defiance, of color bold and free,
Rise up old Thrift to reclaim the land, from sea.
Rooted ever deeply into the ground of thee,
With swords of green upright for battle, Thrift shall ever be.
—An original poem by Roy Heizer

Variegated Oat Grass

Oat Grass comes in both a variegated and an all green variety.

Variegated Oat Grass is often used as a substitute for Liriope.

Variegated Oat Grass is a clump-forming, ornamental grass for cool season gardens or planters. Whirled mounds of foliage lend texture and variegation to the northern New England coastal area. An excellent choice for small urban beds and containers, Variegated Oat Grass is stunning as a single specimen or as a companion to other cool-season, bedding flowers. Variegated Oat Grass is on display throughout the gardens of Portland, Maine, and Portsmouth, New Hampshire. A two-season, perennial ornamental, Variegated Oat Grass returns in early spring, goes dormant in hot weather, and returns for a fall showing once the temperatures have cooled off for the season. The flowers of Variegated Oat Grass are considered insignificant by most gardeners, who plant it for texture, form, and its ability to spread.

Oat Grass is native to most of Europe. It was incorrectly placed in the true Oat family, Avena Sativa, by Carlos Linnaeus around 1755. This Swedish botanist created the bi-nomial system of nomenclature, or two-name, naming system for scientific identification in the 18th century. The mistaken nomenclature placement was eventually corrected, but the common name, Oat Grass, remains in wide use by gardeners. The species type is all green, with variegated varieties being developed in the latter half of the 20th century.

Asarum Europaeum
Wild Ginger

A shade loving woodland perennial, Asarum is easy to grow in the wild garden.

This woodland groundcover is somewhat rare in the cultivated garden, but is slowly coming into fashion. Gardeners in the northeast are discovering how easy *Asarums* are to grow, and what benefits they bring to the shady, moist border. The *Asarums* Dutchman's Pipe style flower is fascinating, sensitive and short lived, lasting only a few days. Most gardeners will not even notice the flowers, as they are borne under the leaves and hidden from view. Wild Ginger is best known and utilized as an evergreen foliage, groundcover planting.

Asarums provide a unique textural element to deliberate undergrowth, displaying tightly arranged round or cupped leaves to contrast sharper margins. The low-mounding leaf bundle will spread by rhizomes, but are not considered invasive. Gardeners have several varieties to choose from, with the shiny, dark, green-leaved types being the most common.

The *Asarum Europaeum* is not the culinary Ginger of the family *Zingiberaceae*, but the rhizome is considered to be useful for medicinal purposes by Native Americans. Wild Ginger has an emetic effect and has also been traditionally used by Native Americans as a cathartic. This use is derived from the herbal medicine tradition and its employment is strongly discouraged.

In the Islamic tradition, wild plants such as Ginger are a metaphor for a person whose righteousness is obfuscated and whose heart is better than their appearance. For example; a Wild Ginger may not appear to be consequential, when in reality it is a plant of great value.

Pawpaw or Poor Man's Banana

A North American native, Pawpaw has a long tradition in American folklore.

Many gardeners say that Pawpaw fruit tastes like banana.

What gardener doesn't remember "The Pawpaw Patch Song," an old-fashioned, traditional folk rhyme;
Where, oh where is dear little Danny?
Where, oh where is dear little Danny?
Where, oh where is dear little Danny?
Way down yonder in the paw-paw patch.

Come on girls, let's go find him,
Come on girls, let's go find him,
Come on girls, let's go find him,
Way down yonder in the paw-paw patch.

Pickin' up paw-paws, put 'em in your pockets,
Pickin' up paw-paws, put 'em in your pockets,
Pickin' up paw-paws, put 'em in your pockets,
Way down yonder in the paw-patch.

Where, oh where is dear old Nellie?
Where, oh where is dear old Nellie?
Where, oh where is dear old Nellie?
Way down yonder in the paw-paw patch.
—Author unknown

This beloved folk song was about the fruit produced by the *Asimina*, the Pawpaw. A favorite fruit of Indigenous Peoples, its native range spreads from Delaware, Maryland and New Jersey in the east through the Mid-west. A holarctic tree, the *Asimina* can now be found growing in half of the states in America. An under-story tree for rich bottomlands, the Pawpaw is very sensitive to full sunlight, preferring shade. Pawpaw fruits are the largest edible fruit native to America, and can be eaten fresh, right off the tree. The fruit of the Papaw Tree is roughly the shape of a kidney bean, but about the size of a grapefruit.

The *Asimina* tree has large, tri-lobed leaves that reveal its family connection to the tropics and explain the botanical name, *Triloba*. Unlike its tropical relatives, the Pawpaw Tree is deciduous. In time, the *Asimina* can grow to around thirty feet in height and is widely known to sucker profusely. Rare in the modern urban landscape, Pawpaws can still be found in the wild throughout the United States.

Barberry or Japanese Barberry

Barberry is available in burgundy, green, and candy-stripped varieties.

A Japanese native, Barberry grows wild across regions of the Appalachian Mountains.

Sprawling branches and burgundy-colored leaves have made Barberry a favorite ornamental landscape shrub in recent years. Gardeners and landscapers should, though, use caution in the placement of Barberries. All Barberries, regardless of variety, have wicked anti-social thorns along the length of the slender arching stems.

In its native Japan, Barberry grows rapidly in semi-open woodlands and sparse, rocky hills. In America, Japanese barberry has become naturalized all over the northeast and has been classified as an invasive species in Connecticut and Rhode Island.

River Birch and
Paper Birch or White Birch

B

Betula Nigra

Betula Papiafara

The beloved, American poet, Robert Frost, wrote of the *Betula Papyrifera* in his famous poem "Birches," and the Birch tree has been held in high regard among poets and the literary class ever since.

Traditional Pagan folklore holds that because of its spiritual qualities, as well as its association with the underworld, Birch branches can be used to exorcise evil spirits by waving the twigs in the air around persons needing help. In that same tradition, it's said that tying a green sash around a branch of a Birch tree will ward off evil curses. Religious scholars of the Pagan tradition note that Birch wood was once used to make baby cradles, as the Birch wood was thought to provide protection to the infants in the cradles as they slept.

The Birch is also associated with the tradition of Astrology. In this tradition, Birch represents those born in December. Birch people, as they are called in Astrology, are perceptive, imaginative, kind, honest and fun loving. Unfortunately, they are also known for being argumentative, impulsive, and prone to flights of fancy. Historically, Birch people were superstitious and would take pieces of the *Betula* tree to wear around their necks to ward off these negative factors.

Hardy Orchid or
Chinese Ground Orchid

Bletilla Striata is a favorite of southern gardeners who now live in the north.

Is there a hardy orchid for the mid-Atlantic and the Northeast? Yes, there is! Gardeners in zones 6 and 7 no longer need to envy the ability of Southern gardeners to grow orchids outside, year round. Showing off sword-like leaves and bright lavender to pinkish purple flowers, the Chinese Ground Orchid is a reliable pseudo-bulb perennial for Northern Orchid enthusiasts. The Hardy Orchid, a terrestrial or ground growing member of the *Orchidaceae* family, displays several flowers per upright stem in the warmer summer months. The overall size of the Hardy Orchid can vary, depending on species, with an average height of 8 to 9 inches.

A hardy ground orchid, this purple flowering perennial, is proof that even northern gardeners can have a tropical flair.

Mulch Chinese Ground Orchid in winter to keep the roots warm.

Borage or Starflower

Beautiful blue star shaped flowers are a hallmark of this historic garden plant.

B

A native of Syria, Borage is a freely self-seeding, annual herb that grows throughout the northern hemisphere. Although technically an annual, Borage acts as a perennial and will return with a new generation, from seed, each spring. Ornamentally, a blue, five-pointed, star-shaped flower is the hallmark of Borage. Blue is a somewhat rare flower color in the American landscape, and many gardeners plant Borage for the diversity of color it brings to the ornamental bed. Borage is covered almost entirely in fine, hair-like pubescence that conveys a pleasant, ornamental effect. The leaves are large, rough, and irregular in appearance, while the overall plant stands approximately two to three feet tall. A distinct identifying feature is the perfect, five-petaled flowers, which are each backed by a prominent, five-pointed calyx.

In use in America since the 1600s, Borage is today planted in colonial gardens along the east coast due to its historical relevance. Planted and cultivated throughout the years, Borage is considered by most historical gardeners to be the quintessential herb of both colonial and modern gardens.

Borage has been well documented since ancient times, for its use as both a culinary and a medicinal herb. Several recipes from the Middle East utilize boiled Borage leaves. The use

A medicinal herb, Borage has been grown in American gardens since Colonial times.

B

of Borage flowers as a garnish is noted in many table and plate decoration articles. Medicinally, Borage has been utilized in the treatment of hormonal issues, such as pre-menstrual syndrome and hyperthyroidism. A natural oil can be derived from the seeds of the Borage plant. The oil is marketed as "Starflower oil," and is taken as a fatty-oil, dietary supplement.

Brassica Oleracea

Cabbage

Cabbage has been a staple food around the world for centuries.

While most American gardeners think of Cabbage as a boring, but useful, culinary vegetable, it actually has a long history throughout Europe. Cabbage was first introduced to cultivation from wild species that grew in seaside areas across the Mediterranean and British Isles, in the centuries before the Christian era (B.C.E.). Early in human civilization, people began to appreciate *Brassica* and its many cultivars that include cabbage, cauliflower, broccoli, brussels sprouts, kale, and savoy. Cabbage is a winter-developing vegetable, providing both ancient and modern peoples an excellent food source in the winter months. In most cases, the Cabbage head, with its tight whirl of fleshy leaves, is cut whole upon maturity and boiled in water. The boiling method of cooking is most common, and several recipes, including sauerkraut, can then be made with the resulting base. Cabbage heads also can be cut and diced raw, making the main ingredient in coleslaw.

Roman statesman and naturalist, Pliny the Elder, stated in the first century C.E., referring to Cabbage: (translated from the original Latin) "This fleshy head is the greatest of all the vegetables, serving both soldier and civilian, in war and in peace. Its medicinal properties are without compare."

Sauerkraut, made from Cabbage, is a staple in Jewish cuisine.

In England, a head of Cabbage is often referred to as a loaf, while in Scotland the globular head is called *Bowkail*. In the Victorian era *Language of Flowers*, Cabbage was said to represent pride and perseverance.

An easy-to-grow vegetable that is perfect for the harsh, salty and often adverse conditions of the coastal garden, growers from Maine to Maryland can produce (no pun intended) and harvest Cabbage when not much else is happening in the border.

A biennial, Cabbage will flower yellow in its second year, but when grown as a vegetable it is harvested in its first year, circumventing the flowering process. When grown as a vegetable, Cabbage must be newly planted each year, fed regularly with an organic fish emulsion and treated as an annual.

Brunnera Macrophylla
Siberian Bugloss or Bugloss

B

Brunnera, a northeastern favorite, is grown from Maine to Washington, D.C.

A member of the Borage family, Siberian Bugloss is a rhizomatous, mounded flowering perennial. In mid-spring, it has small blue flowers on open, branched racemes that swirl above the foliage on slim, irregular, upright stems. The Siberian Bugloss is often called False Forget-Me-Not, a reference to its strong resemblance to the Genus *Myosotis*, the true Forget-Me-Nots. Blue is a somewhat rare flower color, and Siberian Bugloss is often included for the blue hues it brings to the border. By mid-summer, Siberian Bugloss can reach over 18" tall, but rarely needs staking. When the flowers have been spent by late summer, deadheading will be necessary to maintain a neat garden.

While much is made of flowers in the garden, some perennials are just as noteworthy for their foliage. Siberian Bugloss does, indeed, display fun blue flowers, but its large heart-shaped and softly variegated leaves, with a hint of silver, demand attention. This semi-shade-loving perennial is reliable in zones 3 to 8, thriving in any coastal New England or Mid-Atlantic Cottage or English garden. Gardeners have noted that Siberian Bugloss is deer resistant, while drawing beneficial insects that pollinate the spring border.

Campanula

Canterbury Bells or Bell Flowers

Grown in America all along the eastern seaboard Canterbury Bells were brought to these American shores by early English settlers.

Originally grown in Europe, Canterbury Bells have delighted gardeners worldwide for generations with an array of flower colors. The large, bright flowers of Canterbury Bells are a show-stopper in the cottage gardens of America, England, and France. The bell-shaped flowers blossom in the summer months, peaking at a time when many other flowers are starting to show exhaustion.

In northern coastal gardens, Canterbury Bells are best inter-planted en-mass among shrubs and perennials, thriving in maintained flower beds, wild borders, and containers. Canterbury Bells are biennial plants that thrive in dappled to sunny locations in any sandy garden soil. Biennials are plants that grow on a two-year life cycle, showing vegetative growth the first year and reproductive growth

Enjoy Canterbury Bells in white, pink, purple, or all three.

the second. They often self-seed, therefore acting as a perennial. Campanulas prefer cooler areas and can be found in zones 3 to 7, rarely in zone 8. Gardeners can choose seasonal deadheading to keep the garden neat, but this practice circumvents reproduction and decimates a Bellflower population.

The common name, Canterbury Bells, acknowledges the geographical origin of the species, while the botanical name, *Campanula*, is Latin for Little Bells, a reference to the shape of the corolla. In the *Language of Flowers*, a listing of flower meanings, Canterbury Bells was said to represent gratitude and devotion. Several classic Irish tales mention the Bell Flower, and most of these tales relate the flower's ability to hold a memory.

Trumpet Creeper or Chinese Trumpet Vine

Campsis Grandiflora can be invasive, but is manageable with regular attention.

A close relative of the common American Trumpet Vine (*Campsis Radicans*), Trumpet creeper is a scandent vine with large, outstanding flowers. The flowers, usually a shade of orange or tangerine, are abundant in the summer months. The name Trumpet Creeper refers to the shape of the flowers which are fluted and tubular like the musical instrument. Trumpet Creeper can grow to over twenty feet in length in a single season, climbing or creeping over anything in its path. This vine is generally considered manageable for display in the sunny landscape. The *Campsis Grandiflora*, if situated in a suitable spot, can grow quite large. The Chinese Trumpet Vine is also regarded for its quirky, sharply serrated leaves that develop along the length of its growth.

The Trumpet Creeper is native to Asia, where its large flowers are

A scandent wildflower.

C

associated with all manner of fairies and garden spirits. The following story comes from the Chinese tradition.

There once was a Chinese mother who liked to garden with her daughter, Chunhua. They would spend long summer days planting flowers and vegetables, telling stories and joking around with each other. As the years passed, the daughter grew up, got married and moved to a village several miles down the road. The mother continued to work in her garden and the daughter began to establish her own garden at her new home.

Chunhua loved her husband and relished her new life, but sometimes she missed her mother. The miles kept them apart most years and they were only able to see each other on rare occasions. Chunhua missed her mother even more after her own daughter, Ling, was born. As a baby shower gift, Chunhua received from her mother, a Trumpet Creeper plant. While thinking of her mother, Chunhua planted the Trumpet Creeper on the edge of her garden closest to her childhood village. Chunhua's mother planted a Trumpet Creeper in her own garden the same year to remind her of her daughter and granddaughter.

The two Trumpet Creepers began to grow and grow and grow. Quickly, the two vines met and became intertwined. Legend has it, that to this very day, Chunhua and her mother's spirits travel along the length of the vine forever connecting the mother to her daughter and granddaughter.

Carpinus Caroliniana
American Hornbeam or Ironwood

Hornbeam is a columnar, upright tree native to Europe. It is often used as a structural element in garden designs.

Most Hornbeams have golden bronze fall color.

A medium-sized tree for the native shade garden, Ironwood grows with vigor from Atlantic Canada south throughout New England and the mid-Atlantic region. A relative of the Beech tree, Ironwood is smaller overall, but shares many characteristics with its enormous cousin.

Like many hardwood trees of the forest, Ironwood has many stories and legends associated with it. This story comes from a colonial fishing village in coastal Connecticut. One day, a fisherman was preparing his boats for the coming fishing season. He was cleaning and painting the side of the boat when a stranger walked up to him and said "I'll bet ya your boat that with that yonder tree I can create the biggest vessel you've ever laid eyes on." The stranger continued, "If I fail, ye may have my very life for service to you forever." After some thought,

the fisherman agreed, and soon a new gigantic fishing boat, made from the wood of the yonder *Carpinus* tree, was floating at the dock, ready to make its maiden voyage. The stranger said "I win! Your old boat is mine" and the stranger sailed off in the fisherman's boat. The fisherman stood there staring at the Ironwood boat that the stranger had created out of a single spindly tree, amazed and saddened that he had lost the bet. He did not know what he would do without his boat, his livelihood. Soon though, the giant Ironwood vessel spoke to the fisherman, and said, "The stranger did indeed take your boat, but the stranger left me for you. Go and fish the sea with me, till your new boat runneth over with a massive bounty!" For its solid unbending faithfulness, the fisherman forever called the vessel "Ironwood."

Catalpa
or Southern Catalpa

A large tree with large leaves, Catalpa is a member of the bean family.

Heart-shaped leaves frame beautiful flowers.

Native to the southern United States, Catalpa will grow in Delaware and Maryland, but can be hard to locate. The Catalpa, with its huge leaves and showy flowers, impresses even the most hardened native-tree enthusiasts.

Large, heart-shaped leaves are borne on sprawling branches, while the ruffled blossoms display multiple colors on a bignonia-style flower. The overall shape is billowy and wider than tall, creating a shady spot where a swing or Adirondack chair can be used to sleep away a hot summer day. Catalpas are known for being easy to grow and irregular in shape.

California Lilac or New Jersey Tea

The bushy, open shape of the California Lilac resembles that of an un-pruned Crape Myrtle (*Lagerstroemia*), with a similar flower time and palette. Although the overall appearance of the *Ceanothus* is similar to the Crape Myrtle, the flower shape is quite distinct, having a more tubular structure. The flower color of the *Ceanothus* can range from Cerulean blue to soft pink, depending on the variety. Most types of this North American native shrub are hardy for the northeast under two growing conditions: dry soil and full sun. The common name, California Lilac, refers to the fact that most varieties of *Ceanothus* are native to the west coast, although a few are native to the east coast.

Ceanothus Americanus, native to the northeastern United States and commonly known as New Jersey Tea, was so named during the American Revolution, due to its use as a substitute tea source for the restricted Camellia. The brew made from the leaves of the *Ceanothus* plant was not a true tea, but rather an herbal beverage, as true tea is derived only from the leaves of the Camellia (*Camellia Sinensis*).

Cedrus Deodara

Deodar Cedar

The wood of the Deodar Cedar was utilized in coffin making in Asia.

A native of south-central Asia, Deodar Cedar grows from Tibet to Russia and from China to Afghanistan. It is a large, coniferous evergreen tree reaching over 100 feet in the wild. With an open yet uniform branch structure, Deodar is often confused with the distantly related Canadian Hemlock.

A trusted evergreen in the landscape trade, Deodar Cedar is planted as a structural element for height or points. A fast grower, Deodar Cedar will quickly tower over garden walls while enduring even the harshest coastal conditions. The Deodar Cedar withstands and thrives in sandy soil, brackish water, and harsh winds, making it a good selection for the northeastern coastal landscape.

Historically, Deodar Cedar has been the subject of veneration by various religious sects in its native range. The tall height of this tree was thought by past generations to be able to reach the heavens, and therefore be able to connect the people to the gods that reside in the sky. Several of these peoples even thought that the god Dar resided in the Deodar Cedar, which is where the name Deodar comes from and translates as *Deo* (Diety) and *Dar* (the tribe), which are combined to make the word Deodar.

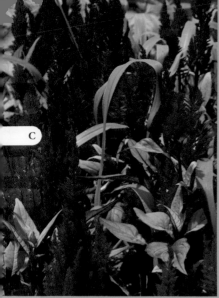

Cockscomb or Woolflowers

Cockscomb adds deep rich colors to the summertime border.

A perennial annual favorite.

A staple in the sunny border, *Celosia* is a flowering annual in the summer color bed. These wildly colorful bedding plants come in a wide spectrum of bright colors and are sought after for their velvety texture. The *Celosia* varieties with a pointed spike-like flowerhead are known as Woolflowers, while the contorted types are commonly referred to as Cockscomb.

Cockscomb, so named for the flowers resemblance to the comb, or fleshy head growth, of a rooster, has an interesting morphology and is somewhat unique among garden flowers. Cockscomb is subject to fascination or cresting, a condition where the flower growth becomes contorted or elongated in irregular patterns. In the case of the Cockscomb, fascination leads to an interesting array of textural developments. Several varieties of plants have the capability to develop fasciation, but the Cockscomb is the most reliable plant for this morphology, which has been bred into it over many years.

The other type of *Celosia* that is planted by American gardeners is named Woolflowers. Woolflowers have a simple spiked flowerhead and come in a variety of bright, clear colors. *Celosias* are generally reliable and easy to care for in the home garden, when given full sun and dry conditions.

Cornflower or Perennial Cornflower

A native American wildflower.

Centaureas' common name is Cornflower, due to its ability to dye cloth a light blue color.

A European native plant, Perennial Cornflower grows with vigor in America and has now escaped cultivation and naturalized here. Both wildflower and ornamental gardeners regard the Perennial Cornflower as one of the most durable and long-lasting flowers in the garden. With both historical and modern uses, Perennial Cornflower can be seen in old fashioned and current landscape designs. It is just as "at home" in historical gardens as it is in urban subdivisions. Perennial Cornflower is also well suited for container gardening, a popular hobby among city dwellers.

In warmer climes, such as Delaware and Maryland, Cornflower is a beautiful upright summer flowering Perennial that brings a unique flower petal configuration to the sunny border. In colder regions of the northeast coast, Cornflower is hardy, but not generally as vigorous. With displays that range in color from all lavender to a deep purple center with white margin petals, gardeners looking to add a royal touch to the color scheme have several choices.

Perennial Cornflower, like many wildflowers, draws several types of wildlife to the natural garden. Companion plants include Black eyed Susan (*Rudbeckia*), Whirling Butterflies (*Gaura*) and the annual Licorice Plant (*Helichrysum*).

Cornflower Blue is a common color used in the clothing and the interior design industries. The original color was made from a dye that was derived from the petals and pollen of *Centaurea* plants.

Chaenomeles Speciosa

Flowering Quince

The Flowering Quince held
magical powers in ancient times.

A medium-sized member of the Rose family, Flowering Quince spends most of the year as a tangled mass of branches and simple green foliage. However, for a few weeks in late winter and early spring, it transforms into one of the most beautiful shrubs in the landscape. Flowering Quince is a deciduous shrub both blessed and cursed with sharp, anti-social, thorny protrusions. The small, simple leaves are arranged alternately on the branches, with a whirled section at each node. Early in the spring season, when few other things of interest are happening in the garden, the bare branches of the Quince are adorned with showy pink to salmon blossoms. The single, semi-double or double flowers can appear in clusters or singly along the stems. In late spring, Flowering Quince develops a small green-to-yellow fruit, that can be made into a jelly or marmalade. Wildlife enthusiasts appreciate the Flowering Quince's ability to attract bees and butterflies to the spring border.

Flowering Quince makes an excellent single ornamental specimen, but can also be used in mixed hedges and borders to great effect. Because of its thorny dense tangle of branches, it also makes an effective security barrier when planted under windows or espaliered against a low wall. In its native Asia, gardeners have worked for decades to select patterns and create hybrids of Flowering Quince that blossom in hues of crimson, rose, and fiery red. Flowering Quince, due to its colors and early blossoming, is one of the most popular selections for bonsai.

Chelidonium Majus
Greater Celandine or Tetterwort

A New England wildflower that bleeds a yellow sap when its stem is broken. Chelidonium is invasive despite its beauty.

A member of the Poppy family, Greater Celandine is native to Europe, where it grows as a cultivated and uncultivated wildflower. In Europe, *Chelidonium Majus* has many herbal and medicinal uses, leading to its colonial introduction to American gardens. Tetterwort can be seen growing wild throughout much of New England and the Mid-Atlantic seaside regions, in open fields and un-maintained lots. While many American gardeners think of Greater Celandine as a beautiful but invasive weed, its medical uses and history are noteworthy to historians and Ethno-botanists.

Greater Celandine must first be untethered from Lesser Celandine, which is a member of the unrelated Buttercup (*Ranunculus*) family. A yellow flower color is the only attribute that Greater and Lesser Celandine have in common.

Greater Celandine is widely known for its dark yellow or orange sap, which has the consistency of liquid latex. When the leaf or stem of Greater Celandine is broken, the sap will ooze out slowly and can be gathered for medicinal or other uses. This Eurasian perennial has been noted among herbalists as a remedy for ailments ranging from Eczema to coughing. Some herbals list its use as a salve for a wide assortment of eye conditions. Pliny the Elder, a Roman naturalist, listed *Chelidonium Majus* in his writings from the first century C.E. Birdwatchers note the use of *Chelidonium Majus* by Swallow Tail birds, and some herbalists refer to Greater Celandine as Swallow Wort.

Wintersweet or Winter Sweet

The common name for Chimonanthus is Wintersweet, due to its winter flowering.

C

Does a fragrant winter-flowering shrub exist in the northeast? Yes, and Wintersweet is living proof that gardeners from Maryland to New York can enjoy year-round color and fragrance in the garden.

Redolent of perfume, Wintersweet gets its common name from the spicy, sweet-fragrant scent emitted by the flowers over the winter months. Flowering from December through February, Wintersweet displays an abundance of small waxy yellow blossoms along otherwise bare irregular upright stems. The drooping waxy flowers of the Wintersweet are able to resist copious amounts of ice and snow, maintaining their beauty

Wintersweet flowers in February and March. It has large green leaves in the summer months.

all winter. Since winter-flowering provides the Wintersweet with no natural insect pollinators, several days after the pendent blossom opens, the Stamens bend over the stigma and the shrub self-pollinates.

A medium-sized, deciduous shrub, the Wintersweet displays a canopy of lush green lanceolate leaves in the summer months. The Wintersweet thrives in part-shade or dappled-full sun in any regular soil. The multi-branched structure provides birds a place for nest building and, therefore, Wintersweet shrubs have become a favorite habitat source for bird watchers. In the landscape, the thickly branched *Chimonanthus* shrub makes a particularly good border for screening streets or neighbors while maintaining an open feel.

Native to China and imported to Iran early in human history, herbalists in western Asia and the Middle East have utilized the Wintersweet shrub for centuries to treat such ailments as bruises, burns, and heatstroke. The Wintersweet was naturalized in Greece early in the Common Era, and the botanical name, *Chimonanthus*, comes from the Greek words for winter and sweet. Wintersweet blossoms have essential oils, derived from the waxy flower, that are used in aromatherapy, cosmetic, and perfume products.

Golden Star or Gold-n-Green

Chrysogonum is a fun colorful bedding plant for the full sun border.

A small, perennial groundcover, Golden Star graces any coastal garden with bright yellow flowers for the entire summer season. Coastal gardens are often sandy, and groundcovers, such as Gold-n-Green, help to stabilize loose soils and stop erosion. The nearly evergreen foliage and stunning flowers of *Chrysogonum* can withstand the sometimes harsh conditions of coastal areas with little adverse reactions. The Genus name, *Chrysogonum*, comes from the Greek words "*chry*" meaning gold and "*gon*" meaning offspring, a reference to the flowers and the seeds.

Legend tells the tale of Golden Star from the perspective of a young Native American girl named Shallow Water. One day, Shallow Water was out in the field picking flowers, with which to make a dye. As she picked the flowers she noticed a boy from her tribe who she had not seen in a while. Shy but wanting to talk with the boy, Shallow Water let some of her flowers catch the wind and float down the field to where the boy stood. Soon the boy, named Swirls-in-Wind, took notice of the flowers and turned to see from which direction they were coming. When he looked up and saw Shallow Water, he forgot about his work, the flowers, and everything else. Swirls-in-Wind simply stared at Shallow Water and she stared back. At last, he picked up one of the flowers that had blown his way and he walked toward Shallow Water. As he approached her, he nervously braided the flower stem in his fingers. When he got to the radiant Shallow Water, he put the flower on her finger and pledged himself to her. She smiled and looked down, blushing. When she opened her eyes she saw the golden flowers flourishing over her fingers. The two youths fell to the ground in each other's arms, only to be covered in a blanket of Golden Star flowers under a brilliantly illuminated sky. Ever since then, Native American folklore has called this flower Golden Star, in honor of Swirls-in-Wind and Shallow Water's love.

Corylus Avellana Contorta

Contorted Filbert or Harry Lauder's Walking Stick

Harry Lauder's Walking Stick gets its common name in honor of Sir Harry Lauder. He was Scotland's most celebrated comedian and entertainer in the early 20th century. He utilized a branch of Corylus as a walking stick in his act.

Serendipitously discovered in a remote English hedge border in the mid-1800s, this six- to twelve-foot-tall shrub has consistently been in cultivation as a contorted version of the European hazelnut since that time.

Planted almost exclusively as a single specimen, the Contorted Filbert has uniquely twisted and spiraled branches, irregular twigs, and leaves. The long, dangling, yellowish catkins are also appreciated for their complementing appearance, although they rarely produce actual Hazelnuts. These characteristics make the Contorted Filbert a unique accent shrub for the full-sun, ornamental display garden. A deciduous shrub, Harry Lauder's Walking Stick's contorted form is most noticeable in winter, when the branches are bare, especially when backlit or under-lit by landscape lighting. In the summer months, a mature Contorted Filbert displays a heavily textured mound of leaves. The rounded, serrated leaves are so dense they completely cover the branch structure, creating a cascade of rich green color. Contorted Filbert is a close relative of the Birches.

Scottish lore says that the Contorted Filbert gained its most famous common name, Harry Lauder's Walking Stick, after the entertainer Harry Lauder, who began to use it in his act as a twisted cane. Inspired by Harry Lauder, many men across the British Isles began to use the branches of *Corylus* as a cane, making it quite the fashion statement in the first half of the 20th century.

Cotoneaster

Cotoneaster is a ground cover shrub for the New England Gardener.

A close relative of the widely known *Pyracantha*, Cotoneaster is a sprawling, prostrate shrub with irregular branching. A ground cover that is often planted on hillsides to help stop erosion, Cotoneaster will creep along an embankment, rooting and continuing to spread as it grows. Though most often planted on slopes, Cotoneaster will thrive in any sunny, dry location regardless of topography. The heavily textured leaves of the Cotoneaster are a glossy, army-green over the summer, developing deep red-burgundy to purple-black fall color late in the season. The small leaves are semi-deciduous, with more than half remaining on the plant over the winter. Cotoneasters are planted by gardeners for use in the winter garden, adding a structural element and visual appeal.

Small white flowers adorn Cotoneaster from mid-spring to early summer. The flowers attract all manner of bees, birds, and butterflies to the coastal garden. Wildlife attracted to the Cotoneaster will find copious amounts of nectar to gather, leaving this shrub pollinated for the coming fall. Late in the summer, the Cotoneaster develops small, red fruit that resembles loosely clustered *Pyracantha* berries.

Cotoneaster is also one of the plants that Ethno-botanists suspect of being among the herbal drawings in the *Voynich Manuscript*.

Crataegus
Hawthorn
or Mayapple

Hawthorn is often used as the root stock for grafted trees due to its adaptability and hardiness.

The Hawthorn is an ancient tree, shrouded in mystery and folklore. A somewhat rare tree in the modern landscape, the Hawthorn was a source of wonder for pre-Christian peoples.

In England, the flowers of the Hawthorn emerge in early May and were once used extensively in "May Day" celebrations. This custom was a celebration of the arrival of the summer months. Similar summer celebrations involving the Hawthorn flower also developed in Scotland, where this medium-sized tree blossoms about two weeks later. In both Great Britain and Ireland, there were superstitions associated with digging up a Hawthorn. The superstition said that anyone who displaced a Hawthorn would himself be displaced for all eternity.

In Ireland, the Hawthorn was considered to have magical powers, and the branches were used to create "scribe sticks" used to write spells, potion recipes and hexes. Despite the nefarious reputation of the Hawthorn in the Britain Isles, it was also viewed as a symbol of hope.

In Celtic folklore, a Hawthorn tree marks the entrance to "the other world," and is always associated with elves, fairies, and sylphs. Celtic folklore says that it brings bad luck to prune the branches of the Mayapple tree at any time of the year, other than when it is in blossom.

In later times, Christian folklore said that the Hawthorn was used in the famous "Crown of Thorns" worn by Jesus at the time of his execution. This is most likely incorrect, as the Hawthorn is a northern, cool, damp-

Both those interested in science and those interested in folklore appreciate the wide spectrum of uses that the Hawthorn offers. This medium sized tree is a classic in gardening circles.

Hawthorn trees are steeped in history and folklore from England and Ireland.

weather plant and would not have been known in the Middle East. It is, though, not an odd suggestion, as many plants have been offered as the plant in that biblical story. The true plant of the "Crown of Thorns" is still a mystery to scholars.

In eastern-European mythology, the Hawthorn is considered especially deadly to vampires, and Hawthorn stakes were prized as the wood of choice for the slaying of the un-dead. This accounting continues with the use of the Hawthorn wood for the coffin of the un-dead, said to keep the vampire down so that its shadow would never again roam the earth to frighten villagers.

A member of the Rose family, the Hawthorn is also sometimes called the Mayapple, as it produces a small *Pyracantha*-type fruit, called a "Haw." The fruit has been a food source for man, mammals, and birds throughout history. Native to northern Europe, Mayapple would have been foraged by Germanic tribes that would also have hunted deer that grazed on the fruit of the Hawthorn. The flowers of the Hawthorn are usually small and white. Borne in loose clusters at the end of branches, the Hawthorn flowers are a good source of nectar for several types of insects, including bees, butterflies, and moths.

Like many members of the Rose family, *Crataegus* are also known for their thorns, hence the name Hawthorn. The thorns of the Hawthorn are not true thorns, but rather sharp, undeveloped branches.

Crocus

Crocus is the first flowering garden plant to emerge in the spring, often pushing up through the snow.

A harbinger of warmer days, Crocus is one of the earliest garden plants to emerge and flower in the spring. Tiny, short Crocus flowers push up through frozen ground and snowpack in early March, at the first sign of the returning sun, telling gardeners of the coming season. Crocus, a member of the Iris family, is a hardy, *cormous* perennial for the northeastern. full-sun border.

Native to much of Europe and Asia, Crocus has been cultivated as an ornamental flower for centuries. In modern time, American gardeners often plant the Crocus among other perennials in order to stagger

Gardeners love the candy-striped varieties.

There's gold in them there gardens!

Crocus is the organic source for the culinary herb Saffron.

flowering times throughout the season. The leaves of the Crocus plant are slender and upright, resembling the distantly related Giant Mondo grass.

A variety of Crocus, *C. Sativa*, is the sole source for the highly regarded culinary spice Saffron. *Crocus Sativa* is native to Asia Minor and dates to around 2500 years B.C.E. Mentioned in both the Bible and Middle Eastern folklore, Saffron is said to be one of the most expensive spices and has, historically, been one of the world's symbols for wealth. It takes approximately 69,000 individual *Crocus Sativa* flowers to produce one pound of Saffron, at a current market price of $5,300 a pound. So valuable was Saffron in antiquity that substituting Turmeric for it was a punishable crime in Germany in the 15th century.

In Greek mythology, Saffron was considered a cure for sleeplessness and an aphrodisiac. Legend tells that Zeus made his bed on a mountain of Saffron, which led to his supernatural powers. During the Dark Ages, Saffron was dispensed medicinally to quell anxiety and reduce fever in patients suffering from nervous disorders. In ancient Egypt, both Saffron and Crocus Sativa were incorporated into pre-Islamic religious services, most likely local King worship.

A staple spice in Middle Eastern cooking, Saffron is used in tiny amounts to add a distinct flavor to both sweet and savory dishes. Arabians utilize Saffron in coffee recipes along with Cardamom. In Spain, Saffron Rice Pilaf is a regular culinary dish that has graced Spanish cuisine for centuries.

Crossandra Infundibuliformis

Firecracker Flower or Freedom Flower

A tender, yet colorful bedding flower.

Crossandra is an annual flower for the northern, coastal, summer garden. *Crossandra* is closely related to the Bear's Breeches (*Acanthus Mollis*), both being members of the Acanthus family. Firecracker Flower produces bright yellow or orange flowers over a whirl of large, shiny, deep green leaves.

Cuphea

Cuphea or Cigarette Plant

Cuphea is commonly known as the cigarette plant or Mexican Heather depending on variety. Wildlife gardeners and hummingbirds alike appreciate Cuphea.

A popular plant among nature enthusiasts, the Cuphea is perfect for drawing nectar-hungry hummingbirds and butterflies to the landscape. The common name, Cigarette Plant, refers to the long, tubular flowers that are a glowing orange or red color and resemble a burning cigarette. The Cuphea flowers emerge from a multi-stemmed whirl of branches in mid-spring and will flourish all summer, dying down only after a hard freeze.

Due to their abundant flower production, Cupheas are also known to attract good spirits to the garden. These spirits are thought to be the ones that bring butterflies and hummingbirds to the flowers.

Gardeners across America appreciate this colorful member of the Legume family.

Cytisus Scoparius

Scotch Broom or Scot's Broom

Native to western and central Europe, Scotch Broom is an upright, multi-branched shrub. The abundant stems are slender, square, and sparsely covered in a whirl of small, linear or trifoliate leaves. Scotch Broom will mature to over five feet in height under ideal conditions that are dry and sunny. This large semi-evergreen prefers full sun and sandy soils at low altitudes, making it an ideal specimen or hedgerow shrub, along the coastal region. The bright, yellow flowers that appear in spring are typical of members of the Legume family.

Scotch Broom is an ornamental, flowering shrub on the east coast, where it is readily planted and not considered a problem. On the northern west coast, however, Scotch Broom is known to be invasive. It is classified as a category-B invasive in the state of Washington, where it is banned from sale. In Oregon, it is also banned as invasive, for pushing out the native species. Though not invasive on the east coast, immature seedpod removal is recommended to gardeners. This quick procedure can be done as soon as the flowers begin to fade in late spring.

Scotch Broom, or Scot's Broom as it is often called in Scotland, is a historically planted shrub well known throughout that country. *Cytisus Scoparius*, or simply Broom, as the British know it, gets its common name from this plant's historical use as a broom. The long, slender, tightly bunched stems, when inverted, work well to sweep floors and dust behind furniture. In Ireland, Broom is said to have spiritual power; spirits of the dead can be caught in the branches when the plant is waved in the air. Once enveloped in the stems of the Broom, those spirits can then be directed to perform tasks for the living. This ritual of spirit commandment has historically been associated with the Pagan tradition and the Scotch Broom is sacred to followers of earth-based religions.

Daphne Genkwa
Lilac Daphne

An early flowering shrub for the New England Coastal garden.

A weather-hardy shrub, Lilac Daphne feels just as "at home" in Portland, Maine, as it does in Dover, Delaware. A spring-flowering ornamental, Lilac Daphne is perfectly able to handle the freezing conditions of zone 5, or the brutal heat of zone 8. This compact, deciduous shrub, with a rounded pleasing form, does best in full sun in the north, while dappled shade is ideal in its southern range.

Small, lavender-to-purple flowers emerge along the stems before the leaves in mid-spring, giving the *Daphne Genkwa* a show-stopping display of Lilac-like flowers. The flowers of the Lilac Daphne emerge in late April in New England and mid- or late March further south. The flowers perform well when cut and used in floral arrangements, adding a flourish of light purple to the spectrum.

Ghost Tree or Dove Tree

The Ghost Tree, a tree with
a haunted history.

The original, scientific description of *Davidia Involucrata* dates back to the mid-19th century. It was first recorded in western China, along the trade routes from Europe to Beijing, in the remote lowlands of Yining. Now known to be related to Black Gum (*Nyssa*) and Dogwood (Cornus) trees, *Davidia Involucrata* was once a mysterious tree displaying dangling, ghostly forms that played into the superstitions and religious beliefs of the locals. One such story about the Ghost Tree comes from that region.

Chinese folklore relates that in the lowland region near the lakes was a cemetery where, over the years, many people were buried. Poor working farmers and laborers from the nearby villages all were brought to the graveyard upon their death. A beautiful, sturdy tree began to grow near the center of the graveyard, but none of the locals knew the name of the tree, only that it's eerily enchanting form was watered with the tears of the bereaved. As the skeletal branches spread out over

the tombs in the burial yard, it was noticed by a visiting father that the tree had become possessed of ghostly spirits. The man believed that the floating white apparitions were unearthly entities of those buried there. Nearly consumed with fear, he told his neighbors of the small, white, ghostly spirits that lilted ominously among the crooked branches of the mysterious tree.

As the story of these spooky apparitions was told and retold, the tree became known as The Ghost Tree. It was thought to be a place where those in the spirit world came and went from the other side of life. In time, the ghostly stories took on religious meaning, and it came to be believed that the Ghost Tree acted as a Psychopomp for the recently deceased. Eventually, families of the interred would visit the tree on the anniversary of a death, hoping they might commune with the spirit of their departed, floating among the branches of the Ghost Tree.

In time, *Davidia Involucrata* seedlings were planted around the region and the tree took on different meanings in other places. It was later given the common name Dove Tree, due to the large white bracts' resemblance to wings and tail feathers of a dove. In recent years, the Dove Tree has become an ornamental specimen across Europe and Asia, with introduction to the American landscape in the last quarter century.

Edgeworthia
Paper Bush

Flowers slowly emerge over several weeks on this difficult to grow plant, rewarding its owner's patience.

A specialty specimen, the Paper Plant is native to Asia.

A relative of the Hollyhock, Paper Bush is a somewhat rare shrub in the Delaware and Maryland garden. A winter-flowering shrub, the fuzzy white buds of the Paper Bush open to a pale yellow in January or February. The winter flowers are set on quirky and bare branches that are appreciated by gardeners, until late spring when lush lanceolate leaves envelope this medium-sized shrub. Difficult to both find and grow successfully, the Paper Bush is regarded among landscapers as a specimen plant for collectors.

The name Paper Bush comes from the *Edgeworthia*'s traditional use in the making of paper products in its native Japan.

Enkianthus or Bloodbells

An upright deciduous shrub, Enkianthus reminds southern gardeners of the Crepe Myrtle in form and size.

Beautiful dangling bell-shaped flowers and brilliant fall color are the Enkianthus' two best attributes.

An ancient legend tells the tale of how the *Enkianthus* came into existence, and how it became known as Bloodbells. Centuries ago, a young man named Ian and his young lady, Enka, took long, romantic strolls along the beaches and inlets of eastern China. The two young lovers would listen as the temple bells rang harmoniously over the hills. Ian, a tall slender man, would often comment to Enka how beautiful he thought her hands were, and how they reminded him of the lush foliage of the nearby forest. Soon though, Ian and Enka were noticed by Dapri, a mysterious and jealous man from the village. Dapri wanted Enka for himself and set about getting her, with no regard for her or Ian's feelings and wishes. Dapri was cunning and deceitful, laying traps for the two lovers. When, after several tries, Dapri was unsuccessful in enticing Enka, or at least dissuading Ian, Dapri planned an attack.

One night, while Ian and Enka walked in the bright moonlight along the beach, a chill began to roll over

their shoulders and the once-bright night began to darken. In a swirl of sand, Dapri appeared before the two lovers. With a flash of silver metal, Dapri slashed into Ian, whose blood spewed forth splattering onto Enka. As Dapri continued to wield his steely jealousness, he cut deep into Ian. The open wounds splashed bloody red all over the coastal area. Enka leaned over the dying Ian and cried many tears of sorrow upon his mortally wounded body. But in killing Ian, Dapri also killed Enka, as she died from heartbreak on that beach. Upon seeing what he had done, Dapri fell to the sandy shore, shriveled up like one of last year's leaves, and rotted back into the ground.

As for Ian and Enka, the legend says that wherever a drop of Ian's blood splattered, an Enkianthus shrub sprouted and the brilliant splays of fall color represent the blood that Ian shed for love. According to the legend, the abundant flowers of the Enkianthus are forever to be shaped like the bells from the temple, soaked in Ian's blood and Enka's tears. The *Enkianthus* is, to this day, said to be the embodiment of Ian and Enka's love. This legend is the source of the botanical name *Enkianthus* and the common name Bloodbells.

Epimedium
Barrenwort or Fairy Wings

Small white flowers and stunning coloration have made Barrenwort a garden favorite since colonial times.

Barrenwort has a long history as a medicinal herb.

A hardy and reliable herbaceous groundcover, Barrenwort is fast becoming a regular in coastal area gardens from Maine to North Carolina. Barrenwort is a semi-shade-loving woodland perennial that fits into any northeastern garden design plan, thriving in zones 4 to 8. The low-mounding leaves are Cordate, or heart shaped, with color that varies with the temperature from lime green to pale yellow and is imbued with blood-red veining. The flowers of Barrenwort emerge in early spring in shades of white, yellow, and pink. By mid-summer, the flowers swirl above their clump of foliage in open clusters, resembling Whirling Butterflies (*Gaura*). Early planters of Barrenwort noted the four-petaled shape and floating motion of the flower, and began to call it Fairy Wings, and that common name has been used ever since. The flowers last until late summer, while the foliage remains a subtle, color-changing show-stopper until the second or third hard frost.

Sea Holly

Globe Thistle has recently become popular with American coastal gardeners, but folklore stories surrounding it have existed for centuries.

Sea Holly is a prodigious, thistle-like perennial in the coastal garden. The upright stems of the Sea Holly hold stiff, circular, umbrella-style flowerheads that are almost always bluish lavender to purple. This plant always maintains a rosette of rounded, simple leaves at the base, while the leaves along the main stem develop spiky, anti-social characteristics. In a dry, sunny location, Sea Holly will spread slowly to fill a small space.

The *Eryngiums* are a member of the *Apiaceae* family, making them a close relative of carrots, celery, and Queen Anne's Lace. *Apiaceae* members are noted for their aromatic qualities and for having a hollow stem.

The common name, Sea Holly, comes down through the ages and is associated with Pagan traditions. The Sea Holly tells the story of a small village and a battle between the Holly god (the god of winter) and a large sea creature. In the year 3000 B.C.E., a small village on the coast of Persia at the Gulf of Oman was being ravaged by a sea creature named Udkla. The villagers thought that they were being attacked by Udkla, because they were not venerating the god of winter sufficiently. They set out to procure a Holly tree for worship; a large Holly tree was located and planted in the center of the community. Soon, Udkla attacked again and the villagers cut Holly branches to use as weapons against the great creature. When Udkla approached the village, the people furiously thrashed him with the Holly branches and the mighty Udkla was killed. As Udkla lay dying, the villagers looked down at their Holly branches and saw that they were not Holly branches at all, but the stems and flowerheads of the *Eryngium* plant. The villagers forever called the plant Sea Holly, in honor of the Holly god who helped them to be victorious in battle.

Eucommia Ulmoides
Hardy Rubber Tree

E

Eucommia Ulmoides, or Hardy Rubber tree, is not related to *Hevea Brasiliensis*, the true tropical Rubber Tree or to *Ficus Elastica*. It does, however, produce rubber. In its native China, the rubber-like sap of the Hardy Rubber Tree has been tapped for centuries in the making of industrial products. Additionally, Chinese herbalists have listed *Eucommia* among Chinese medicinal herbs for millennia. The bark of the Hardy Rubber Tree can still be found in some Chinese herbal markets.

In America, the Hardy Rubber Tree is planted as an ornamental shade tree, lauded for its ability to withstand winter temperatures into the minus 30°F range. The city of Boston, Massachusetts, has planted several Hardy Rubber Trees along the waterfront greenway. A medium-sized deciduous tree, Hardy Rubber Tree creates long-lasting shade and natural beauty in the urban environment.

Burning Bush or
φλεγομενος θαμνος

Burning Bush create outstanding hedgerows as they mature.

Burning Bush is widely planted for its fall color.

Widely planted for its outstanding fiery-red, fall color, Burning Bush grows with ease from Maine to Maryland and beyond. The Burning Bush, in fact, gets its common name due to its fall color and reminiscence of the biblical story of Moses.

Burning Bush, a multi-stemmed deciduous shrub, is a pleasing but nondescript border hedge over the summer months. Burning Bush tops out at over 6' tall and wide, with thick, solid branching in an overall fountain-like form. It is ubiquitous in the sunny American landscape for its use as a barrier hedge, though many landscapers display it as a single specimen.

A native of Greece, *Euonymus Alatus* has historical roots in the Mediterranean region, where it has been growing wild and under cultivation for many generations. The second botanical name *Alatus* is Latin for "winged," a reference to the long, corky ridges of bark that run along the length of the many, squarish stems. The bark, from an angle, resembles a silhouette of wings. The Latin word *Alatus* is also the root of the word Altitude.

Hearts a Bustin' or Strawberry Bush

Hearts a Bustin' is a woodland favorite in shady coastal regions.

All Euonymus are originally native to Greece.

E

A spindly, vine-like shrub, *Euonymus Americana* is one of only a very few *Euonymus* species native to America. The vast majority of *Euonymus* species are indigenous to Greece. Found growing wild from central New York southward to Florida, Hearts a Bustin' is a wonderful addition to any native or wild garden.

The leaves of the Strawberry Bush reveal its familial connection to the genus Euonymus, bearing a strong resemblance to other members of this family. Sometimes lost among other foliage in the summer border, Hearts a Bustin' leaves begin to reveal amazing fall color as the weather cools, displaying a golden, honey-russet pallet with a hint of lime.

Gardeners will notice a dangling, strawberry-like fruit pod that appears at about the same time as the fall color. The reddish-pink seed pod, the size of a dime, looks similar to a human heart. In late December or early January, the heart-like pod opens forcefully, ejecting one to four small, bright-red seeds, hence the common name Hearts a Bustin'. After the seeds have been pushed out, the pod turns an almond-brown color. The seeds attract both birds and viewers to the native garden. This plant will perpetuate by seed in the untamed garden, but is not considered invasive and is a valuable addition to any northeastern coastal, winter border.

European Beech or Common Beech

Fagus is in the Oak family.

The European Beech is steeped in medieval folklore and mythology.

center of veneration since before the Common Era. It is and has been widely worshiped for its massive size, whereby it reaches into the sky and mingles with the clouds.

The Common Beech, at maturity, reaches over 100' x 60', with a bole circumference that can exceed 20'. The trunk is a light, ghostly gray that is mostly smooth, but can occasionally have warts and irregularities. Finely serrated, the leaves are a glossy, dark green, with 10 or 11 leaf veins that draw directly out from the mid-rib in rigid order, an identifying feature for the Common Beech. The leaves turn scarlet red and burgundy in the fall, later turning light brown and persisting on the branches through the winter.

An important tree, both historically and culturally, the European Beech is commonly found in mixed-hardwood forests and landscapes on both sides of the Atlantic ocean. A close relative of the Oak tree, the European Beech has a long and interesting history in the traditions of religions. In the ages before skyscrapers were built by man, hardwood trees were the tallest things on the earth, and the European Beech has been the

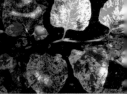

Fallopia Japonica

Knotweed or Japanese Knotweed

Unique variegation patterns are the Knotweeds' hallmark.

Japanese Knotweed

Growing throughout the American northeast, Knotweed is a beautiful, invasive, ornamental plant native to Japan. It is so invasive that it has been banned in several counties in New York and Pennsylvania. In the counties where it is permitted, gardeners regard Knotweed as suitable only for wild areas and natural gardens that are maintained regularly. Japanese Knotweed is an herbaceous perennial vine, or upright grower, that dies down in the winter but comes back with vigor each spring. The slightly triangular, heart-shaped leaves and small, white flower clusters are two of its best attributes. Knotweed can be found in its natural, all-green variety or in a variegated hybrid form; it can be seen as a vine or as a stalk-forming, tall perennial. As a houseplant, Knotweed is more manageable, but will attract the curiosity of cats.

In Japan, the local religion Shinto, or Shintoism, holds the Knotweed in high regard. Shintoism says that as long as the Knotweed grows, Kami will live. Kami is the main spirit in Shintoism, and several Japanese native plants are associated with the Shinto faith. In the loosely related faith of Buddhism, Knotweed is known to be strung as living garlands on the Emu stand.

Fescue or Tall Fescue or Kentucky 31

A Kentucky native,
but well suited to the northeast.

A premier lawn grass in the American northeast, Tall Fescue is actually a flowering evergreen, native to Europe. It was first introduced to American soil in the 1940s as a ground cover. Tall Fescue is a cool-season grass that remains green all winter, as opposed to warm season grasses that are dormant and brown during the colder months. Fescue Grass is not heat-resistant and fairs poorly south of zone 7. Suited for the sun or shade, Tall Fescue is a medium-textured, thin-bladed member of the grass family *Poaceae*, one of the world's largest plant families that includes Bamboo, Barley, Corn, Palm trees, Rice, Rye, Sugar Cane and Wheat.

Unlike a Bermuda Grass lawn that spreads on stolons, a Fescue lawn is made up of many individual plants bunched tightly together. Gardeners and landscapers appreciate the well-behaved Fescue that will not run up onto sidewalks or over flower beds.

Broadly appealing for its resistance to disease, Tall Fescue is also durable and easy to maintain. When properly and regularly cut to a height of 2", an established Tall Fescue lawn does not need any auxiliary water from a sprinkler. In fact, over-watering is the primary accelerant of lawn diseases. Occasional and judicious hand-watering during periods of drought will produce the best results. A balanced, organic fertilizer, applied once a year in the late summer, will help the grass to have the nutrient supply it needs over the winter.

Forsythia or Border Forsythia

One of the first flowers to emerge in spring, Forsythia is well known for the explosion of bright, golden yellow blossoms that cover the long, leafless stems. When winter dormancy dominates most other shrubs, Forsythia is enticing gardeners back to the garden to prepare for the coming season. The small, star-shaped, yellow flowers tend to come out during an early warm spell and, unfortunately, they are often burned back by continuing frosts. If the weather cooperates, Forsythia flowers last for weeks, adding brilliant color to a bleak landscape that is still waiting for spring.

Later in the spring, the Forsythia flowers are overtaken by the emerging leaves that are clear green, heavily serrated and strongly veined. The leaves appear in opposite pairs at each node where the flowers were once held. By early May, the leaves are fully out in most of the northeast and this shrub has gone from a golden yellow to a rich green. The overall shape of the Forsythia

Along with Crocus, Forsythia flowers are one of the first garden colors to appear in the spring.

is upright to arching, and "fountain like" is how most landscapers describe its appearance.

A multi-stemmed shrub that can reach 6' in height and width, Forsythia should never be pruned except to clean up dead stems. Normally very hardy, Forsythia stems are hollow and harsh pruning allows cold winter air to reach the roots. This cold air can freeze and kill the root system of the Forsythia.

Border Forsythia prefers cooler northern locations and is hardy in zones 4 to 7a. The Forsythia is not fussy about sunlight or soil, thriving in all but full shade. This shrub may be easily propagated by gardeners through layering, a technique that involves laying stems that are still connected to the mother plant to the ground (usually with a rock or brick) until they root. Rooting takes one season, at which time the newly rooted plant may be cut off from the mother shrub and re-planted.

A native of China, the Forsythia is the subject of an ancient creation story from the western part of the Qinghai province. In the narrative, the Forsythia is seen as a giant spider that represents the creation of the universe. As the spider grows and reaches out, with its many legs across space, it puts down contact that creates its own life or planet. In time, all the planets grow and flower. The flowers, in turn, represent life on earth. In this story, the branches of the Forsythia are seen as spider legs and the propensity of this shrub to root upon ground contact is the development of the universe. In folklore stories, flowers often represent life.

Witch Alder or Witch Wand

F

Fothergilla is a spring-flowering shrub that is native to eastern America. Its puffy, brushy, and rounded white flowers emerge in April or May and persist through the summer. *Fothergilla* can grow to a height of seven feet, and is a favorite among native plant enthusiasts for its longevity. The *Fothergilla* has a stout, upright heavily branched structure and should never need pruning. Witch Alder is a natural or woodland shrub, but can be grown successfully on the Atlantic coastal plain. They are slow growing and gardeners need to be patient with them until they develop. The flowers of the *Fothergilla* attract all manner of wildlife, including bees and butterflies. Bird watchers appreciate the many types of birds that are drawn to the *Fothergilla*, including cardinals, mockingbirds, and robins. *Fothergilla* is also grown for its outstanding fall color. A medium green over the summer, the heavily textured leaves turn many shades of red and salmon in late September and early October. In some species, swirling hues of yellow and gold compliment the reds.

Fothergilla gets its other common name, Witch Wand, from an old farmers' folklore tale that relates it was once used by witches of the meadows to make their wands. Being in the *Hamamelis* family, Witch Wand is a close relative of Witch Hazel, and many stories surrounding them have been used interchangeably. There is also mention of forest elves using the Witch Wand as a rod or staff, to drive out unwanted spirits from the trees.

European colonists took the *Fothergilla* back with them to Europe as early as 1690, and they can now be seen occasionally in gardens along the coasts of France and Spain. *Fothergilla* is rare elsewhere in the world.

White Ash or American Ash

The classic Ash tree.

An American native hardwood tree, White Ash grows abundantly from Atlantic Canada, down the east coast and across the eastern United States. An incredibly uniform tree, White Ash has a wide columnar bole with dense, straight-grained wood. The bark and branches are both noted for being rigidly standardized, with a rounded, full, overall shape. Rarely found in pure stands, White Ash is most often found in mixed forests that also contain Beeches, Maples, and Sweetgums. White Ash now averages 70 to 80 feet at maturity, while older natural specimens have measured at over 100 feet tall.

A wonderful landscape tree for larger areas, White Ash are strong, fast-growing and long-lived. A White Ash tree provides shade in the summer that cools a home and garden, while also providing habitat space for wildlife. The opposite pinnately compound leaf configuration of the White Ash gives the northern gardener textural diversity in the greenscape. It is noted by native tree enthusiasts and landscape designers for its deep burgundy to russet-red fall colors, which are rich in tone and clear in presentation. The fall color pallet is not typically considered flashy, but is reliable even under less-than-ideal weather conditions.

Colonial settlers in the thirteen original colonies would have used the wood of the White Ash for several purposes, including construction materials. White Ash planks and frames can still be found today in some historic colonial homes in the northeast.

White Ash is widely used in commercial products as a renewable resource. The White Ash is noted in the wood industry for its ability to be sanded, polished, and to take stains and varnishes, as well as its minimal shrinking and warping. Due to its strong, straight-grained wood, White Ash is used in the production of baseball bats and the handles of good-quality tools. It is also, occasionally, utilized in the making of high-end, hardwood floors, mantles, and other finishing-trim details.

Sweet Woodruff or Lady's Bedstraw

Pilgrims and other early colonist in America would have known Galium as bed straw.

An upright groundcover perennial, Sweet Woodruff flowers in spring in semi-shade, woodland settings. The slim, erect stems have small clusters of star-shaped flowers at the tips, while whirls of lance-shaped leaves emerge at each node along the short, herbaceous shaft. Sweet Woodruff, a pleasantly scented spreader, will fill-in ground spaces between *Enkianthus* or Rhododendrons without aggressively taking over other plantings. This plant is occasionally referred to as *Asperula Odorata*, and some confusion exists among botanists and taxonomists as to the true nomenclature. An especially hardy and adaptable perennial, Sweet Woodruff graces gardens from Maine to Maryland, where it was a staple herb in colonial gardens.

In Victorian flower symbology, white is often the color of peace, surrender, or tranquility. Sweet Woodruff flowers have inspired many works of art from the British Isles, and Sweet Woodruff bouquets are shown in paintings, place settings, and wallpaper designs throughout Europe.

The botanical name *Galium* comes from the Greek word for milk, *Gala*. In ancient times, cream was curdled with *Galium*, as a form of Rennet, and utilized in the production of cheese.

In Christian folklore, a tale from Medieval times relates that Lady's Bedstraw was used in Jesus's cradle. According to the legend, coarse straw was the only material in the barn where Jesus was born, so Mary and Joseph went outside and picked *Galium* herbage. The soft, flexible foliage and pure-white flowers became the bedstraw for the baby Jesus, and *Galium* was known forever afterwards as Lady's Bedstraw.

Kentucky Coffee
Tree bean.

Once the state tree of Kentucky, the Kentucky Coffee Tree is a large deciduous tree in the mixed hardwood forest. The profuse white, star-shaped flowers are borne in mid-spring on the tips of the branches, and develop into a multi-podded fruit set after pollination. A slow growing but competitive tree, the Kentucky Coffee Tree has a naturally occurring range stretching from Maryland and Tennessee in the south to New York and Michigan in the north. Autumn color on the Kentucky Coffee Tree can range from bright, clear yellow to a muted butter with russet hues.

The Kentucky Coffee Tree is not common in its native range and was first described by early settlers who learned about it from the Native Americans. Many years before English and European colonists settled the eastern shores of the United States, Native Americans gathered the beans of the Kentucky Coffee Tree, roasted them, and produced a bitter, coffee-like drink. While the settlers drank the beverage out of a sense of communion with the Native Americans, the Kentucky Coffee Tree drink was never their "cup of tea," and the settlers dispensed with its use as soon as regular coffee began to be available.

Native plant landscapers and specialty gardeners have begun to plant the Kentucky Coffee Tree in upscale gardens, native plant gardens and botanical conservatories. Several growers around the northeast and mid-west are beginning to grow this unique flowering tree on a large scale for landscape use, insuring the survival of this historic species.

A member of the *Fabaceae*, or Pea family, the Kentucky Coffee Tree is closely related to alfalfa, beans, carob, licorice, peanuts, and peas. The Kentucky Coffee Tree is also related to Scotch Broom (*Cytisus scoparius*) and Kudzu (*Pueraria lobata*). The *Fabaceae* family is, after the grass family, the most agriculturally significant plant family in the history of mankind.

Hamamelis Ssp.
Witch Hazel

Witch Hazel is a winter flowering shrub. It has brightly colored strap like petals between December and March when it is bare of leaves.

Beware the ghouls when planting Hazel!

A somewhat rare, winter-flowering shrub, Witch Hazel is most common in natural native gardens and wild areas. A deciduous shrub, Witch Hazel flowers profusely in the coldest months of the year, when the arching branches are bare of leaves. Depending on cultivar, the flowers of the Witch Hazel can range from pure yellow to deep red, with all flowers appearing in a crinkled, "Strap star" configuration. The *Loropetalum* is a close relative, and the two have similar flowers.

The common name Witch refers not to Halloween witches, but to the middle-English word Wiche that means "bendable" or "pliable." The English word "Wicker" comes from the same word, as the branches of the Witch Hazel have historically been utilized in the construction of wicker furniture. Hazel is a common name for the Genus *Corylus*, making Witch Hazel a close relative of the Birches, Contorted Filbert, and *Loropetalum*.

Along with other members of the Hazel family, Witch Hazel has historically been used as a divining rod. The strong, yet flexible, branches were held out at arm's length as the holder walked across a field. When a source of underground water was reached, the tip of the Hazel rod would dip down as an indicator. Where the rod indicated water, a well was dug, with almost complete accuracy. It is a mystery of the Hazel whether the accuracy of the divining rod method is science or magic.

Hosta or Plantain Lily

An American garden classic since the early 1800s, Hosta is actually native to northeast Asia. The Hosta is an easy-to-grow, shade-loving perennial that forms whirled clumps of large, simple leaves that come in a variety of leaf sizes and variegations. A low-growing, herbaceous perennial, Hosta is planted most often as a groundcover, but occasionally as a single, ornamental specimen. The center of Hosta produces multiple stem spikes that hold white- to light-lavender-colored flowers. Like most perennials, Hosta dies down in the winter months only to return in the spring. A good choice for the shady, low-maintenance garden, this plant needs only be cut to the ground each November. Hosta can easily be divided and replanted any time of year.

In Japan, Hosta is called *Giboshi* and its flower is associated with peace, tranquility, and persistence. In its native range, Hosta grows outside cultivation and is therefore Japan's most widely recognized wildflower. The entire plant is edible and, while American gardeners tend to avoid eating it, the Japanese consider *Giboshi* to be a regular part of their diet. *Giboshi,* or Hosta, is a close relative of the vegetable asparagus.

Humulus Lupulus

Hops

Hops are one of the main ingredients in the brewing of beer. There are both ornamental and culinary varieties of this sprawling bine.

Both green and yellow cultivars of Hops are available.

Hops are most widely known as an additive to flavor and stabilize beer. When used as an ingredient, Hops gives beer its bitter flavor and Hops-drying houses can be seen throughout the northeastern United States, as well as across Europe. Gardeners, however, grow Hops as a vigorous twining perennial bine that can grow over twenty feet in a single season. A massive bine by summer's end, Hops will completely overtake a tree or fencepost if not maintained. Large, heavily textured, green leaves with distinct, serrated margins are the foliage hallmarks of Hops. The flower is pine-cone shaped and dangles in loose clusters at the ends of the many stems. The flowers of *Humulus Lupulus*, which start out green and mature to a light brown color, only develop on female plants and are the source of the ingredient for beer production.

Hops grows at a rampant rate once it emerges in early spring and can cover a porch, trellis or pergola by the end of July, particularly at the southern end of its range. *Humulus Lupulus* is technically a bine, and is different in its morphology than a vine. Hops are not invasive and will never escape into the wild. Hops prefer full sun and rich organic soil, but will adjust to poorer soils if given fertilizer and regular watering. The vegetative growth will die back to the ground each fall, and gardeners will need to cut it back to retain a neat garden appearance. Hops cuttings are a good source of nutrients, and composting the clippings will enhance the garden's value each year. A reliable perennial, Hops will return from the roots each spring.

Peegee Hydrangea

The Peegee Hydrangea is one of the most useful plants in the northern coastal border, with flowers, color, form, and hardiness leading a long list of attributes.

The early-emerging leaves of the Peegee are smaller than other Hydrangeas, and their clear, matte-green color provides this shrub's flowers with a natural canvass over the summer months. The small, quad-petaled flowers of the Peegee develop in early spring in tightly clustered balls, which are numerous.

Gorgeous white flowers in summer, outstanding fall color, tree or shrub form, usefulness for crafts and arrangements, and ability to withstand zone 3 winters are just a few of the Peegee Hydrangea's many attributes.

Hydrastis Canadensis

Golden Seal or Yellow Root

A rare but treasured woodland perennial
with large leaves and raspberry-like fruit.

H

Native to the northeastern United States and Canada, Golden Seal is a shade-loving, perennial herb for the woodland garden. Its most distinguishable identifying feature is the single white flower that develops into a rapsberry-like fruit in mid-summer. The bright red berry sits above a slim, single stem, over large leaves that are reminiscent of the Acanthus. Golden Seal is a very hardy native, growing vigorously where winter temperatures can dip below freezing for extended periods of time.

Hydrastis Canadensis spreads by rhizomes, and will eventually form a colony. Yellow Root is considered endangered, and its inclusion in the traditional and modern garden is encouraged by native plant enthusiasts. Folklorists claim that it is a shelter for woodland spirits, who feed on its red berries in the summer and follow its roots to the underworld in the winter.

Golden Seal is listed as an herbal remedy in many natural medicinal recipes. Its use as an anti-inflammatory is Golden Seal's most sought-after, herbal attribute.

Candytuft

When in full flower, Candytuft appears as if it is covered in snow.

One of the most durable performers in the garden, Candytuft has earned its reputation for being a hardy, long-lasting, perennial groundcover. An evergreen in zones 7, 6, and 5b, Candytuft will return year after year, all the way to zone 3. Spilling over walls and bluffs, Candytuft provides mounds of pure white flowers from March until June and again, briefly, in the fall. The flowers present in multiple corymbs, giving the plant a mounded, flowing effect when planted en mass. Candytuft needs little care in a well-drained, mostly sunny location and requires no other maintenance beyond mulching to look great year-round. When utilized as a container planting along with other selections, Candytuft provides trailing white flowers to the mix.

Candytuft is native to the Iberian Peninsula in southwestern Europe, which includes Andorra, Portugal, and Spain. The genus name, Iberis, refers to this native range. The second part of the botanical name, *Sempervirens*, translates from Latin as evergreen: *Semper* means always and *Virens* means green. Iberis Sempervirens grows wild on rocky bluffs, as well as the lower elevation of coastal areas, across southern Europe and has been naturalized throughout much of the United States.

The Candytuft name refers not to a sweet treat, but to Candia, an area in the Mediterranean where it grows as a wildflower. This perennial was first referred to as Candy Turf or Spanish Tuft when it became cultivated as an ornamental in Europe during the late 16th and early 17th centuries. It was one of the first ornamentals brought to Colonial shores in the 1600s. Candytuft was planted, by the mid-1700s, in all thirteen original colonies where it is still growing today.

Itea or Virginia Sweetspire

A northern and southern favorite.

An old-fashioned shrub, the Virginia Sweetspire has been delighting gardeners year-round for generations. A native of the Commonwealth of Virginia, the Virginia Sweetspire was named for its spire-shaped flower inflorescence that emits a sweet, but low key, scent. There are several varieties of Itea and the overall shape can vary from species to species. Some Iteas are tall and upright, while other varieties are small and weeping. Some varieties of Itea remain in clump form, while others spread out forming colonies that can eventually fill a small garden. The Itea is easily dug up and transplanted to a different location; they are an ideal shrub for plant swaps.

In the spring, Virginia Sweetspire has an abundance of scented white flowers that emerge from the ends of the branches, while the new spring leaves are an enchanting lime green. Over the summer, the Virginia Sweetspire grows rapidly, developing large, simple leaves and a multi-trunk form. As winter approaches, the Itea shows off a wild, motley display of stunning fall color. Deep burgundy, red, yellow, lime, and orange are just a few of the colors displayed for weeks, from September to November. Even in the dead of winter, the Virginia Sweetspire has an interestingly textured, exfoliating bark to show off along the length of its branches. Gardeners are becoming increasingly interested in winter gardens that rely on form and texture, and the Itea makes a wonderful winter garden specimen.

The Itea has historically been planted in the gardens of many of America's colonial homes. Several old-growth specimens can be seen in Washington, District of Columbia; Baltimore and on many of the historically significant plantations and estates along the mid-Atlantic coast. Delaware and coastal New Jersey display some of the largest and oldest Virginia Sweetspires in America. The Virginia Sweetspire can also be seen as single, ornamental specimens or large hedgerows throughout Delaware, Maryland, New Jersey, and New York. The Itea will also survive winters in coastal New England, if they are planted in a protected area.

Itea, like many plants, will grow well in both the southern and northern coastal regions of America. The Virginia Sweetspire was also featured in this book's companion volume, *Coastal Garden Plants: Florida to Virginia*, by author Roy Heizer.

Jasminum Nudiflorum
Winter Jasmine or Jasmine

The cascading form of the *Jasminum Nudiflorum* can often be seen trailing over retaining walls. It flowers in the cool spring months.

Bright yellow, winter flowers and a cascading appearance are the hallmarks of Winter Jasmine. While most other flowering shrubs are dormant, Winter Jasmine gives the bleak frozen garden a tidal wave of small, clear, yellow flowers that light up bluffs, hills, and retention walls. Able to withstand snowpack and heavy ice, Winter Jasmine is a must for the winter landscape. Even the botanical name, *Nudiflorum*, refers to the winter flowers; translated from the Latin, *Nudi* is nude or without leaves and *Florum* is flowers.

Mountain Laurel or Calf-Kill

Widely known as a mountain plant, Mountain Laurel grows in abundance along the New Hampshire and Maine coastlines.

The state flower of both Connecticut and Pennsylvania, Mountain Laurel is a showstopper in any native garden. An old-fashioned flowering shrub, Mountain Laurel has been grown for its colorful and unique, bowl-shaped flowers for generations. The color palette for Mountain Laurel ranges from white to deep, reddish-pink, with distinct contrasting slash marks inside the single flower petal.

Mountain Laurel is native to the eastern United States, with a growing zone ranging from southern Maine to Florida on the east coast and extending west to Mississippi. While the name Mountain Laurel implies that it will only grow in the mountains, it flourishes throughout flatter, wide-open places, along the northeastern seaboard. The Mountain Laurel is a large evergreen shrub that matures to heights over seven feet tall and wide. It is not a fussy plant, requiring little care after establishment.

In a Native American folklore story from Connecticut, the Mountain Laurel is called Spoonwood, because tribesmen would craft spoons out of the wood. Given that Spoonwood is toxic, this is likely just lore, rather than fact. The story more likely relates the idea that the wood of the Mountain Laurel is able to be carved.

The entire shrub is poisonous to both farm animals and humans. It has been known to kill sheep that graze on it, leading to the names Calf-Kill and Sheep-Kill. Gardeners need to heed this when making planting choices.

Lamiaceae Leonotis
Lion's Tail

An annual for the northern garden.

A very tender perennial or annual in the Mid-Atlantic garden, Lion's Tail is a tropical perennial that has been adopted by many northern gardeners for its bright orange flowers. Northern gardeners with greenhouses or conservatories can grow Lion's Tail with ease, adding a Caribbean feel to a plant collection.

A close relative of Jerusalem Sage (*Phlomis*) and a member of the Mint family, *Lamiaceae Leonotis* displays stunning bright orange flowers. The tight outward-reaching flower clusters are spaced at distinct intervals along the length of the three-feet-tall, upright stems, similar to *Phlomis*. The long leaves of Lion's Tail resemble those of the Spirea, although the two are unrelated.

The common name, Lion's Tail, is due to its resemblance to the tail of the lion. Leon is the Latin word for Lion and the last botanical name, Leonotis, assigned by the Linnaeus binomial system of nomenclature, points out this plant's association with the largest cat.

Bleeding Heart or Old Fashioned Bleeding Heart

Although it looks delicate, Bleeding Heart is very hardy and reliable in the Connecticut and Rhode Island gardens, as well as points north.

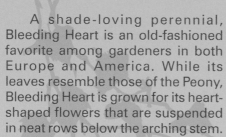

A shade-loving perennial, Bleeding Heart is an old-fashioned favorite among gardeners in both Europe and America. While its leaves resemble those of the Peony, Bleeding Heart is grown for its heart-shaped flowers that are suspended in neat rows below the arching stem.

Bleeding Heart flowers come in white, pink, or red. Despite a delicate appearance, Bleeding Heart is a robust perennial in New England and Mid-Atlantic gardens. Easily able to withstand the coldest winters and the hottest summers of the northeast, Bleeding Heart looks great year after year, with very little fuss. *Lamprocapnos Spectabilis* thrives in any regular garden soil in zones 3 to 8 and is a companion plant to Hostas and Sweet Woodruff. The common name, Bleeding Heart, comes from the heart-shaped flower that seems to have a blood drop dangling beneath it.

In folklore, Bleeding Heart flowers are often associated with loss or heartbreak. They are used alternately to represent the end of a relationship or the healing from one. One such story suggests that, upon getting a broken heart, one should plant Bleeding Heart in the garden to signal the world that, though heartbroken, love is worth trying to find again.

Larix Ssp.

Larch

Strictly a northern tree, this pine family member barely tolerates the Massachusetts summer.

A pine tree native to Japan.

L

A member of the Pine family, Larch is strictly a northern conifer. Growing from Massachusetts northward into Canada, Larch is a winter-hardy tree or shrub that suffers in the heat. Larch is found over half of the Canadian and Russian Taiga, and seen in the wild across Siberia and the Alaskan tundra.

The needle-like leaves come in spirally arranged bundles of twenty to thirty. Larch is the only conifer that displays leaves in that morphology. The cones of the Larch are small and rather slow to mature, resembling Hemlock cones upon development. Similar to the Bald Cypress (*Taxodium*) in the south, Larch, although a conifer, is deciduous. The fall color is a golden yellow to light honey-coffee, depending on variety.

In Scotland, the Larch is the tree of choice for the traditional sport, Tossing the Caber. A 17'-long Larch log is lifted and tossed in the sport, a throwback to Scotland's lumbering days, when Larch trees were used to make makeshift bridges on logging sites.

Wild Rosemary or Ledum or Marsh Tea

Don't mistake this white flowering shrub for Rosemary; they look very similar, but are two different species.

Ledum Palustre flowers resemble Spirea flowers, while the leaves and structure strongly resemble common Rosemary; but *Ledum Palustre* is actually a member of the Rhododendron family. The fragrant flowers of the *Ledum*, which blossom in mid-spring, are white, with the faintest hue of pink on the petals. The multiple flower clusters on this northern native are a strong attractant to bees and other beneficial insects. *Ledum Palustre* requires full sun and moist conditions, and is perfect for the New England seaside garden. A northern plant suited to colder climes, *Ledum* will grow, but suffers, in the heat of the mid-Atlantic garden.

An herb, *Ledum Palustre* has historically been utilized for its homeopathic qualities. An herbal brew can be derived from the leaves of the Ledum, and its introduction into folk medicine dates back generations. The common name, Marsh Tea, refers to its use as a medicinal tonic.

Gardeners familiar with *Ledum Palustre* often plant it to challenge beginners into learning an important lesson: that just because a plant's leaves and shape resemble a certain plant does not mean that it is that plant. All plants are categorized by how they reproduce, and so flower familiarity is essential to plant identification.

Coast Leucothoe or Coast Doghobble

Native to the Mid-Atlantic region, Coast Leucothoe is a small- to medium-sized flowering shrub for the part-sun border. A motley and heavily textured sprawler, Coast Leucothoe provides the seaside gardener with year-round interest. It can be utilized equally well as a single specimen or in mass plantings, to maximize its natural effects.

In the spring, small, white flowers droop down in a loose display along zig-zaged stems. The blossoms are borne under curved lanceolate evergreen leaves that are strongly arranged in a uniform pattern, emerging in opposite sets of two at every leaf axis along the wandering stems. The botanical name, *Axillaris*, comes from the word axis, and refers to the leaf arrangement. New leaf and stem growth is light-wine color, which matures to deep green over several weeks.

In the summer months, Coast Leucothoe adds textural diversity to the mixed shrub border, and this bush is often planted alongside *Pieris Japonica*, as the two shrubs have similar qualities. With a proper water supply, the flowers of the Leucothoe will last until the hottest days of late July. The leaves quickly show desiccation in drought conditions, but regain turgidity once water is supplied.

Perfectly suited for coastal conditions, the Coast Leucothoe is deer and salt-spray resistant. Care of the Coast Leucothoe is generally minimal, as it needs only constantly moist, well-drained soil in part sun. An organic fertilizer, applied in early spring and late summer, will help the Coast Leucothoe preform at its best. Gardeners may choose to clean it up through deadheading in late summer. An evergreen in zones 6 and 7, the Coast Leucothoe is hardy to zone 5, but in that zone will need to be cut to the ground due to winter damage, returning with vigor in the spring.

Honesty or Annual Honesty or Money Plant

Money, Money, Money!!!

Honesty makes an excellent dried flower for ornamental arrangements.

A biennial, *Lunaria Annua* is an old-fashioned garden plant for northern and southern coastal regions, grown for its colorful flowers that emerge in spring and last well into the summer months. This garden favorite is also grown for its unique seed pods. Profuse, oval, and translucent, the seed pods of Honesty are covered in a silvery sheath. In light, the dried seed pods glow like silver coins, hence the common name, Money Plant. Clusters of the dried seed pods were and are highly valued for dried flower arrangements. Historically, Honesty's silver coins were one of the first plants used for making household arrangements. Stored in dry-to-low-humidity conditions, Honesty seed pods can last indoors for years.

A biennial is a plant that has a two-year life cycle. Biennials usually grow and flower their first year, then seed, and die their second year. Gardeners know not to deadhead biennials, as this ends the seeding process. Most biennials self-seed, therefore acting as a perennial even though technically they create a new generation every two years.

In the days before dried flower arrangements were so readily available, home gardeners grew Honesty for indoor use. Decorative vases filled with Honesty were particularly popular at Christmas and New Years. The "coins" of Honesty would have historically been given to Jewish children as gelt during Hanukkah. In the months after the holidays, the vases filled with Honesty arrangements would have given a home a festive feel through the winter. In more recent times, there has begun to be an interest in the winter garden, and the seed pods of the Honesty plant can look wonderfully attractive in an otherwise bleak winter garden. Honesty blossoms in rich purples, pinks, and fascinating bi-colored variations, which are lambent at sunset. A North American native, Money Plant supplies plenty of nectar to bees and butterflies. It is easy to grow and reliably self-seeding in almost any regular coastal garden. Money Plant is a good choice for a child's garden, as it gives young gardeners a two-year project.

Clubmoss

Club Moss

Ancient woodland plants, Clubmosses have intrigued and enchanted naturalists for centuries. Clubmosses are low-growing, evergreen, vascular colonizers that are distantly related to ferns, *Selaginella* and other prehistoric plants. They do not flower, rather, like ferns, they develop spores for reproduction. The Clubmosses' spores develop on "battle club"-looking structures at the tip of each shoot; the common name, Clubmoss, is derived from this reproductive structure. They can also spread vegetatively on subterranean roots. Clubmoss is an excellent example of a whirled-leaf arrangement, with small pointed leaves encircling the upright stem.

Extremely rare in the landscape and garden center trade, Clubmosses are occasionally found at quality plant swaps and through high-end, specialty websites. Most often, native plant enthusiasts simply enjoy them in their natural setting, unutilized woodland forests. Just a few miles inland from the coast, in the eastern foothills of Maryland,

New York, and Pennsylvania, Clubmosses grow in abundance as terrestrial groundcovers. In the wild and in cultivation, Clubmosses are companion plants for Bloodroot, English Ivy, and Ferns.

In millennia past, Clubmosses were held in high regard by Native Tribes that used them for medical purposes. The Clubmoss spores were mixed with mud and applied to bruises and sore muscles. The Clubmoss plant tissue was eaten as greenery, or used to line beds of small animals in domestication.

In Pagan tradition, Clubmosses were held sacred for their wartime symbology. The Clubmoss was viewed as a symbol of the battle club, a wartime weapon. Pagans in ancient Europe believed that if the Clubmoss was given the proper veneration by people, the Clubmoss would transform from a symbol of victory to actual victory in battle. Recently, archeologists have found traces of *Lycopodiaceae* spores in armor from the Middle Ages; it is thought that the Clubmoss was put on armor to bring victory to the wearer.

Magnolia Stellata
Star Magnolia

Winter flowering member of the Magnolia family.

M

While most plant enthusiasts know the Southern Magnolia as a large evergreen, the Magnolia family includes many members that are deciduous shrubs. *Magnolia Stellata*, though, is the "Star" among this branch of the Magnolia family.

Star Magnolia is a large, winter-flowering shrub that blossoms in February or March, before the leaves emerge. Pure white, five- or six-petaled flowers are the hallmark of this Japanese hybrid. The botanical name *Stellata* is Latin for star, a reference to the shape of the flower.

Malus

Crabapple or Wild Apple

Crabapples have been a part of domestic culinary and cultural life for millennia. The history of Crabapples as a cultivated fruit dates back to the Stone Age. Later, evidence of Crabapple fruit was found in coffins from Denmark dating to around 1500 BCE.

Copious amounts of history and folklore surround the Crabapple tree. While some of this history is thought to be fun, parts of it are much more sinister. In England, people once believed that Crabapples had magical powers and that witches sought them out in order to use that power. Witches were suspected of putting potions and poisons into Wild Apples in the hope that people would then use the fruit in their Wassail.

Crabapples, in Europe, were thought to house spirits, and a legend from France relates that if one falls asleep under a Crabapple tree, the person will be protected from evil spirits while they sleep. According to the fable, if the sleeper is harmed while under the tree, the tree is to be cut down and its branches burned. In Spain, Wild Apples were thought to bring bad luck to anyone who would eat them. This legend explains why Wild Apples are almost completely absent from Spanish cuisine. In the Christian tradition, the Apple is thought to be the forbidden fruit from the Garden of Eden story,

Crabapple photographed in Portland, Maine.

The Crabapple is a traditional flowering/ fruiting tree for northern gardens.

although Ethnobotanists find this unlikely. When shown in Adam's hand, the apple is a symbol of sin. When held by Jesus, the Apple represents attractiveness of salvation.

During colonial days in America, native Crabapple trees were utilized by New England settlers for their fruits. Ethnobotanists believe that as early as 1695, cultivated Crabapples were being brought to Massachusetts from England and hybridized with the native stock.

Low Flying Cypress or Siberian Cypress

An extremely rare find in American gardens, Low Flying Cypress is a native of Eastern Siberia, Russia. Hardy to zone 3, this evergreen member of the Cypress family is able to withstand the harshest winters of the coastal Maine and New Hampshire landscape. A rich green color in the summer season, the tightly whirled leaves of Low Flying Cypress turn a dark, reddish burgundy in the winter. Slightly taller than the usual groundcover, Low Flying Cypress forms waves of Cypress-like foliage in thick, low hedgerows. Landscape designers and plant growers in Maine, New Hampshire, and Massachusetts are beginning to appreciate *Microbiota Decussata* for its hardiness and plethora of foundational uses.

The surface limbs conceal a mass of tangled branches below the foliage that provide year-round habitat for all manner of wildlife. It is important for gardeners in the colder climes of New England to provide winter habitat space to squirrels, chipmunks, birds, and insects. The garden critters, in turn, pollinate and sow seeds for the coming season.

In its native Russia, Low Flying Cypress is thought to conceal garden spirits under the protection of its branches. These garden spirits are said to watch out for the gardeners who tend the earth. The spirits are also said to defend the garden from bad spirits, therefore raising the next season's yield.

Muscari Armeniacum

Grape Hyacinth or Common Grape Hyacinth

A small, but persistent, perennial, Grape Hyacinth is prolific throughout the northeastern region. Gardeners plant this reliable spring-flowering bulb for its fragrance and cobalt blue color pallet. Grape Hyacinth will naturalize and colonize quickly, in any regular garden soil, provided it is a dry winter location. Long wandering paths of Grape Hyacinth are often planted to achieve the effect of a river in themed landscape plans. They are also planted in difficult areas where other plants find it hard to develop.

The multitude of Grape Hyacinth flowers are borne on short upright inflorescences, held above strap-like foliage. The individual flowers are tiny, roundly bell-shaped, and fluted. The common name Grape Hyacinth refers to the overall appearance, with the flowers resembling bunches of grapes and the structure resembling that of the regular Hyacinth. Muscaris are a close relative of the Scillas, and gardeners have noted the similarities.

Muscari Armeniacum is native to Armenia, along the border between the Middle East and Asia. In addition to being utilized as a cut flower in its native Armenia, Muscari is also the source for a blue dye that resembles Indigo.

An old Armenian legend says that Muscari is the source of healing from depression. In the legend, Muscari starts out a pale sad blue, with flowers that droop downward. In the end, the Muscari turns drooping flowers into a bouquet of beauty for all generations to esteem. Due to its admirable qualities, some folklorists say that Muscari is the source of "Royal Blue."

Myosotis Sylvatica

Wood Forget-Me-Not

A light blue bedding flower.

Hardy from gardening zones 3 to 9, Wood Forget-Me-Not is one of America's best flowering perennials for adding blue to the color pallet. Wood Forget-Me-Not's primary identifying feature is its yellow center, consistent across all cultivars.

With its consistent five-petal configuration, Wood Forget-Me-Not is the subject of a fun children's game, named "He loves me. He loves me not." The game, if started on "He loves me," will always end in "He loves me."

Narcissus
Daffodil

Daffodils are a traditional spring flowering perennial in both the northern and southern garden.

According to Greek Mythology, Narcissus was the son of the river god Cephisus and the nymph Liriope. In the legend, Narcissus was said to be a handsome young lad, so handsome in fact, that whoever saw him fell in love with him. Narcissus, though, conceitedly shunned the lustful admiration of those around him. One day, Narcissus set off to go hunting in the woods, where he was followed by an Oread named Echo. She too, had fallen in love with the vain, yet beautiful, Narcissus. Unable to speak first, Echo waited until Narcissus spoke out, asking "Who's there?" but she was only able to reply "Who's there!" Upon revealing herself to Narcissus, he rejected her, preferring his own company and leaving her to disintegrate from heartbreak.

Nemesis, the spirit of revenge, saw what Narcissus had done to Echo and sought to exact payment from Narcissus for his arrogance. According to the story, Nemesis guided Narcissus to the edge of a pond and made him become thirsty. When Narcissus bent over the water to take a drink, he saw his own reflection. He instantly and hopelessly fell in love with his own beauty. In the narrative, he stooped to kiss this beautiful and perfect man, not realizing that he was pressing his lips against his own image. So long did he kiss his reflection, he drowned in the water.

The botanical name Narcissus is derived from this story from Greek Mythology, a reference to the ability of someone to get lost in the flower's beauty.

seen pushing up through the snow along with Crocus. Daffodils come in several color and size variations, all of which naturalize quite well in the mid-Atlantic area. Gardeners who plant one bunch of Narcissus will quickly have many clusters of this carefree bulb perennial popping up around the garden. Gardeners do not consider Daffodils invasive, and treat them like beloved wildflowers.

Originally, Daffodils, a bulbous wildflower native to much of Europe, were cultivated from wild specimens in pre-Victorian times and have been grown in English, French, and Spanish gardens for their ornamental value ever since. In Wales, Daffodils are known by the name "Peter's Leek." Daffodils were imported to American gardens in colonial days.

One of the first flowers to emerge in early spring, Daffodils can often be

Narcissus has inspired poets, painters, and songwriters for centuries. Daffodils can be seen in many museum paintings by famous artists. Poets from William Wordsworth to Robert Frost mention Narcissus in their writings. In modern pop culture, folk rock groups ranging from Widespread Panic to The Indigo Girls have also referenced Narcissus in their songs.

Love in a Mist or Love in a Tangle

This Middle Eastern native brings unique beauty
from Syria to the American coastal garden.

Love in a Mist has one of the strangest morphologies in the garden.

Nigella, a flowering annual in the Buttercup family, has been grown in English cottage gardens since the 1570s. It was almost immediately established in American colonial gardens, planted here as early as the 1650s. The *Nigella*'s roots, however, stretch much further back into human history, as the botanical name *Damascena* suggests. *Nigella* is native to Damascus, Syria, and other parts of the Middle East. Philip Miller, an ethnobotanical writer from England, mentioned in his 1760 Herbal text, referring to *Nigella*, "This plant grows naturally in the corn fields about Aleppo, from whence the seeds were first brought to Europe." Aleppo is the largest city in Syria, and one of the oldest in the world. Few flowers can boast of being, literally, from the cradle of civilization.

The one-inch-wide flower of Love-in-a-Tangle is one of the most awe-striking in the ornamental garden. The Sunflower-like circumference of the petal arrangement is backed by a tangle of thorny growth that remains in place after fertilization. A fountain of pistils and stamens erupts from the center of the petals. The short-lived flowers come in an array of colors, including blue, lavender, and white. Gardeners are generally able to accept the short flower time in lieu of the strange and fascinating structural attributes that Love-in-a-Tangle brings to the sunny garden.

The fruit of the *Nigella*, a balloon-type capsule, is composed of five or six attached follicles, each fruit capsule containing several seeds. The capsule is surrounded by a tangle of gnarled, thorn-like protrusions. In the late summer, the fruit capsule opens and releases the seeds. The capsule then becomes dry and brown and is sought-after for use in dried flower arrangements. This strange morphology is the exception to the rule for the rest of the Buttercup or *Ranunculus* family. Though technically an annual, the *Nigella* self-seeds quite readily in the coastal garden, and will therefore act as a perennial with a new generation emerging each year.

Native to Atlantic Canada and all of New England, the Cinnamon fern will enchant native plant enthusiasts and casual observers alike. Cinnamon Fern is one of the largest colony-forming ferns in the northeastern forest, found in shady, low-lying areas from the coast inland.

Like all ferns, the Cinnamon Fern does not produce flowers, but rather develops a large set of fertile fronds and a large set of sterile fronds on the same plant. The fertile fronds are shorter, upright and usually gathered in the center of a whirl of sterile fronds. The fertile fronds dry and turn a cinnamon color, hence the name Cinnamon Fern. The dry, fertile fronds resemble a dried flower inflorescence. All ferns, including the Cinnamon, produce spores, which are nearly microscopic. These spores are spread on the forest floor to ensure the next generation of Cinnamon Ferns. The fronds of the Cinnamon Fern are quite large and arching, with a medium-lime-green, summer, color palette.

Cinnamon Ferns are deciduous and die down each winter, only to return with vigor the following spring. The fall colors of the Cinnamon Fern are quite outstanding and include hues of brown, cinnamon, gold, honey, and yellow. Companion ferns include the Autumn Fern (*Dryopteris Erythrosora*), Hay-Scented Fern (*Dennstaedtia Punctilobula*) and Ostrich Fern (*Matteuccia Struthiopteris*).

Paeoniaceae
Peony

Native to China, the Peony is a reliable May flowering perennial in Maryland and New Jersey.

The Peony is a northern garden favorite and one of its most reliable perennials. The Peony has become an old-fashioned, flowering plant here in America, and is well suited to the mid-Atlantic's hot summers and cold winters. There are many varieties and colors of Peonies to choose from. Peonies have three main types of flowers: single, double, and full, also known as "Peony style." The leaves of the Peony are upright and strongly resemble those of the Hellebore family, which are quirkily divided and serrated. Peonies are originally native to China, but have been grown around the world for centuries. One legend from China recounts the story of a gardener who loved Peonies.

A Chinese botanist spent his life caring for the Peony plant. He had spent so many years in the company of the Peony plant that he had no friends or family left. As time went on, he became in need of an employee to help him care for his growing collection of flowers. As luck would have it, a beautiful young girl knocked on his door and asked if she could work for him. The botanist was happy to employ her and teach her the ways of the Peony. She was, as it turned out, a perfect student: quick to learn and passionate about flowers. The young girl was of impeccable character, morally honorable and dedicated to both the botanist and the Peony collection.

One day, a long-lost love of the botanist's came to the door for a visit. Wanting to introduce the woman to the young pupil, the

Peony petal configurations are nearly endless.

botanist called to the student, and when she did not answer he went looking for her, but could not find her. He went into the greenhouse to search for her and found her flat against the wall hiding behind a piece of glass in a picture frame. No longer in human form, but now a painting, the young girl said to the botanist, "I did not answer you for I am no longer human, but have become the soul of the Peony." The girl in the painting continued, "Your love warmed me into a human and it has been my joy to serve you, but you now have a real human to love and you no longer need me. Enjoy me as a flower, care for me as your own, but go and love her with all your heart." As the moments passed, the botanist's heart both broke and grew; he returned to his door. With tears of sadness and joy, he invited the woman in. The botanist knew, when the woman said, "I love you. I've missed you terribly and I'm glad to be back with you and your beautiful Peony collection." that the young girl was right to return to a flower.

Boston Ivy

This vine really knocks it out of the ball park.

Draping over many buildings across the northeast like a bright-green cloak, Boston Ivy can obscure an entire edifice in a couple of years. In fact, Boston Ivy is so prevalent on the University campuses of Brown, Columbia, Harvard, Penn, Princeton, and Yale that they are collectively known as "The Ivy League," in reference to this vine that covers many of their buildings. While not exclusive to the Boston area, Boston Ivy gets its common name from its ubiquitousness in the city of Boston, Massachusetts.

A close relative of both the Grape (*Vitis*) and Virginia Creeper (*Parthenocissus Quinquefolia*), Boston Ivy graces buildings from Orono, Maine, to Washington, D.C. A prolific, spreading, scandent vine, Boston Ivy needs no support

to easily scale a brick wall, using its own padded tendrils to grasp the surface. The closely arranged leaves are vaguely reminiscent of Red Maple leaves, with three distinct lobes suspended out from the main stem on a short, arching petiole. Over the summer months, the leaves of Boston Ivy are a shiny, clear green, giving the appearance of a blanket on older specimens. When the weather turns colder in the fall and sunlight is reduced, Boston Ivy leaves begin to turn deep, rich, burgundy red. The leaves, when in full fall color, can display many hues of burgundy, deep purple, lime, orange, and red. Boston Ivy's brilliant display of fall color lasts well into the winter months, and fall color at Thanksgiving time is not unusual. A deciduous vine, Boston Ivy loses

From one of the most educated vines in America, the Ivy League gets its name from this plant covering campus buildings throughout the northeast.

its leaves in winter but continues to display a rugged woody trunk that can get quite thick with age.

While most plant enthusiasts recognize Boston Ivy as a northeastern coastal vine, it is also famously covering the outfield walls at Wrigley Field in Chicago, Illinois. It was planted there in the 1930s, as part of a city beautification project.

Russian Sage

A summer-flowering perennial for New England and Mid-Atlantic gardens, Russian Sage provides waves of bluish purple color to the landscape palette. A tall, upright, finely textured plant, Russian Sage attracts bees, butterflies, and onlookers to both coastal and inland borders. Once mature in mid-summer, Russian Sage develops a woody stem near the ground, while the upper stem and inflorescence remains loose and flexible. It is widely planted for its ability to form colonies that sway and wave in the slightest breeze. The leaves of the Russian Sage are finely serrated, silvery white, and velvety in texture. The soft, wool-like, purple flowers of Russian Sage make a great addition to floral bouquets and dried flower arrangements when used in conjunction with other flowers; Baby's Breath and Lilies compliment Russian Sage especially well. Companion plants in the garden include Black Eyed Susan, Coreopsis, Meadow Rue, and Sweet Woodruff.

Russian Sage is native to southwestern Russia, Afghanistan, Iran, and parts of Turkey. In its native range, Russian Sage has been used medicinally for centuries. In ancient days, tribal elders throughout the Middle East would use the strong fragrance of *Perovskia* to induce a mild state of euphoria. This euphoric state produced a trance that was utilized during medical procedures and religious rituals. Native to historical trade routes that led from China to Europe across the Middle East, Russian Sage was often used as a bartering currency among traders.

The Cork Tree is known for its beautiful gnarled, deeply textured bark.

Amur Cork Tree

Technically an herb, Amur Cork Tree is native to China, Japan, and Taiwan, where it has been used as an herbal remedy for centuries. Amur Cork Tree is a close relative of Rue, in the family *Rutaceae*.

In the United States, Amur Cork Tree is an easy-to-grow landscape tree that is planted more for its bark than its pinnately compound leaves. The bark of the Amur Cork Tree is thick, heavily textured and irregular. As this tree ages, its ever-pulling and stretching, cork-like bark develops deep fissures and furrows that are a prized ornamental attribute year-round. A rather stout tree overall, Amur Cork Tree spreads out massive branches that create, in time, wonderfully shady locations for patios or sitting areas. The fall color is a pleasant, if not extraordinary, yellow hue that is accompanied by small clusters of black fruit. The fruits self-sow and sprout easily, and the Amur Cork Tree is sometimes considered invasive in un-managed areas.

The first botanical name, *Phellodendron*, translates from the Latin as "Love of Trees," while the second name translates as "Like the Amur." *Philo* is the Latin word for love, and *Dendron* is the Latin for tree. The scientific study of trees is called Dendrology.

Phlomis Fruticosa
Jerusalem Sage

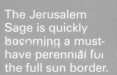

The Jerusalem Sage is quickly becoming a must-have perennial for the full sun border.

A unique flower configuration is the Jerusalem Sage's most desirable attribute.

Displaying one of the most unique flower configurations in the coastal garden, the Jerusalem Sage has caught the attention of gardeners in Maryland, Delaware, and New Jersey. It is becoming an "in demand" perennial throughout the Mid- Atlantic region. The flowers of the *Phlomis* open in a tight whirled pattern around the base of the upright stem; the stem then extends upward and another flower cluster is displayed. This pattern repeats every few inches for the remainder of the inflorescence. The effect, called cluster stacking, is very rare and is therefore quite desirable.

There are several types of *Phlomis* for the landscaper to choose from, and all of them display the cluster stacking feature. Flower colors across the different varieties

include yellow and violet, as well as pink. *Phlomis Fruticosa* is a fun plant for wildlife gardeners as its profuse spring flowers attract bees, birds, and butterflies to the garden. The leaves of the *Phlomis* vary from variety to variety, with some displaying a soft fuzzy texture while others are a simple matte green. All varieties of Jerusalem Sage have opposite leaf arrangement, an identifying feature of the Sage family. Jerusalem Sage is in the Mint family.

The Jerusalem Sage, native to the eastern Mediterranean, is grown in Israel for use in Synagogues as an ornamental decoration. The Jerusalem Sage is a true Sage and has a long tradition in the Israeli garden, where the stacking flower configuration is said to be a building block or ladder to a more peaceful ideal.

Phlomis Fruticosa, like many plants, will grow well in both America's southern and northern coastal areas. Jerusalem Sage was also featured in this book's companion, *Coastal Garden Plants: Florida to Virginia*, by author Roy Heizer.

The Colorado Blue Spruce is slow growing but will reward a patient gardener, with stunning beauty.

Picea Pungens

Colorado Blue Spruce

A strongly pyramidal and uniform evergreen, the Colorado Blue Spruce is one of the most sought-after ornamentals for the northeast landscape. Dense, stiff and reliably silver blue in color, the Colorado Blue Spruce makes a powerful structural statement in the border. Whether planted as a single specimen or in pairs to define an entranceway, the Colorado Blue Spruce is an outstanding addition to the northern coastal garden. A slow growing, but long-lived conifer that eventually reaches over seventy feet, Colorado Blue Spruce is often planted at cemeteries as a memorial tree. *Picea Pungens* is native to the inner mountain west, but despite its roots in the mountains, it grows abundantly in the northern coastal region from zones 3 to 7a.

Gardeners think of exotic plants as being introduced to America, without realizing that some American native plants have been introduced to other countries as exotics there. In the case of *Picea Pungens*, introductions to European gardens started in the first half of the twentieth century. Due to the import trade, Colorado Blue Spruce has now become a regular part of the central European landscape, with outstanding specimens on display in Austria, The Czech Republic, and Germany.

The Colorado Blue Spruce is sacred in mythology of Native American tradition; one such story comes from the northern Rocky Mountains.

The legend tells of two sisters who were being treated cruelly by their stepmother; they decided to

leave their home. Later, they were found by a gentle man who took them in and married them. After some years, they decided to revisit their childhood home, a journey of some difficulty and distance. The good spirits of the Spruce bade them to weave two baskets apiece from needles of the Colorado Blue Spruce, each basket being small enough to fit over the ends of their thumbs. These baskets were to be filled with dried meat and berries. These tiny baskets, holding less than a mouthful apiece, were like the biblical baskets that contained bread loaves and fishes. As the two sisters ate all they wished, along the course of their travels, the supply of food never ceased. When they finally arrived at their stepmother's home after many days, the sisters greeted their stepmother and offered her food from the baskets. The stepmother took of the contents of the baskets without question. Suddenly, the baskets grew to the size they would have been had they contained the food actually used on the journey. The stepmother gorged herself to such a degree that she could no longer breathe. She died in a rapture of gluttonous bliss, and the stepdaughters were avenged.

Aluminum Plant or Watermelon Pilea

Native to Vietnam, the Aluminum is best displayed in the summertime container garden.

A native of Vietnam, Aluminum Plant is grown as an ornamental annual in the summer garden. Frost sensitive, Aluminum Plant thrives in the high humidity and sandy soil of coastal gardens, provided it is in a shady spot. The common name, Aluminum Plant, refers to the striking silver blotches that display shimmering color between the veins of the textured leaves. The flowers of Pilea are small and insignificant, and this plant is grown exclusively for its unique foliage. *Pilea Cadierei* is sometimes known by its alternate common name, Watermelon *Pilea*, an obvious reference to the silver speckles' resemblance to the markings of a Watermelon. A rather small plant overall, the Aluminum Plant makes a good addition to any houseplant collection or garden, when inter-planted among Ferns or Hostas.

Pinus Strobus

White Pine or Eastern White Pine

The White Pine is the state tree of Maine.

The Eastern White Pine grows abundantly from Atlantic Canada to North Carolina along the coast as well as inland.

A stately evergreen, the White Pine is the official state tree of Maine. Although best known as a northern tree, the White Pine has a growing range from Canada to Georgia, along the Eastern Time Zone. White Pine is a very uniform tree, extending branches in a distinctly layered, whirled pattern that leaves the trunk bare in three- to five-foot intervals. Like most Pines, the White Pine does lose its lower branches as it ages. The soft, silvery green needles come in bundles of five.

White Pine is one of the strongest and fastest growing trees in the modern landscape. A favorite of native tree enthusiasts, the White Pine is a good choice for creating a quick evergreen barrier or border on residential lots. *Pinus Strobus* attracts all manner of birds and wildlife. The strong, horizontal branches hold up well under heavy snow pack, creating a picturesque winter scene.

During colonial days, White Pine was used in the ship-building industry to make masts because of their height, strong and flexible wood, and sharp, natural taper.

White Pine is a traditional choice for Christmas Trees, as they hold needles for weeks after cutting. The flexible branches of the White Pine are also used as garlands, strung together to decorate bannisters and fences.

In Iroquois native folklore, White Pine is known to be the "Tree of Peace." In what is now upstate New York, Iroquois would bury weapons under White Pine trees as a symbolic gesture of peace. This action is where the modern saying "Let's bury the hatchet" originated.

A medium-sized tree
grown for its fall color.

The Chinese Pistache is an under-appreciated, medium-sized, landscape tree. Fast growing, strong, and uniform are three desirable attributes of this tree. Its fall color display is one of the most outstanding, with scarlet, reds, and yellows in the natural palette. The bright autumn hues of the Chinese Pistache can be compared only to those of Sugar Maple (*Acer Saccharum*).

Platanus Occidentalis
Sycamore or Buttonwood

Widely known as the Buttonwood Tree, Sycamore is easily recognizable due to its smooth white bark.

Platanus Occidentalis holds a unique place in American financial history. On May 17th, 1792, twenty-four stock brokers gathered on Wall Street, in Manhattan, New York, under a Buttonwood tree, to sign documents that would become known as "The Buttonwood agreement." In short, "The Buttonwood agreement" cut out stock sellers, or auctioneers, as they were called, and set certain rates and percentages. These papers, named for the tree under which they were signed, were the founding documents for what we know today as The New York Stock Exchange. The New York Stock Exchange would not exist had it not been for "The Buttonwood agreement."

While Buttonwood is an accepted common name, most Americans know this tree as the Sycamore. The Sycamore tree is one of the most ubiquitous deciduous hardwood trees in North America, growing from Canada to Florida.

Native to North America and Europe, the Sycamore is a good choice for the native ornamental landscape, provided it is given room to grow. In the modern landscape the Sycamore plays an important role in helping to shade houses and yards. Shade from a tree such as the Buttonwood can cool a house and lower air conditioning needs, saving a homeowner significantly on their electric bills. The shade can also protect lawn space from the hot summer sun, leading to a dramatically reduced need for sprinkler system watering and extended usage of lawn areas. Hardwood trees like the Sycamore also reduce noise and air pollution in urban areas, leading to a more comfortable lifestyle.

The Sycamore's most widely recognizable feature is its bark. The exfoliating bark peels off in light gray fragments, showing large spots of smooth white trunk and branches. A massive and fairly uniform tree, the Sycamore can grow to well over eighty feet tall and wide. It develops seed clusters that are about the size of a golf ball and are persistent through the winter. The leaves of the Buttonwood are also noteworthy for their size and distinct shape, being among the largest in the American landscape.

Podophyllum Peltatum

Mayapple or American Mandrake

A woodland perennial, Mayapple has a long history in the Native American tradition.

Peltatum refers to the way the leaf is attached to the stem like an umbrella.

A woodland perennial, Mayapple grows wild over much of the northeastern United States, from Maine to Maryland and west to the Mississippi River. With a height of less than two feet tall, Mayapple would be easy for naturalists to miss were it not for the distinctive leaf pattern that makes this plant so interesting. The leaves come in two distinct shapes: a full roundish umbrella and a divided, dual, half-umbrella form. The flower forms only on the divided leaf forms. The last botanical name, *Peltatum*, refers to the umbrella-leaf style, botanically known as Peltate.

Found both in small groups and extensive colonies, Mayapple inhabits undisturbed, deeply shaded woodland areas where large, hardwood trees protect them from the harsh summer sun.

The single Mayapple flower is held out on a slightly drooping stem under the divided peltate leaf. The flower petals are fan shaped, small, and pure white.

Poliothyrsis Sinensis
Fall into Spring

A Chinese native, *Poliothyrsis Sinensis* is a large, fall-flowering shrub for the ornamental border. Rare in America, *Poliothyrsis Sinensis* grows in coastal gardens from Boston to Baltimore, where it extends the flowering season into the fall. From September until Halloween, *Poliothyrsis Sinensis* displays loose panicles of small, white flowers at the ends of upright, irregular branches. A deciduous shrub with distinctive bark, *Poliothyrsis Sinensis* displays its multitude of whirled, sculptural branches throughout the winter months. In the spring, heart-shaped leaves emerge in a color pallet of mauve, soft yellow, and russet, that more closely resemble fall colors than spring. The petioles stay distinctively red all season, while the leaf blades mature to a rich green for the summer months.

The common name, Fall into Spring, is derived from the unusual fall flowering and the even more unusual spring leaf colors. Gardeners and landscapers seeking unique specimens should consider the ornamental value, ease of care and zone 6 and 7 hardiness of Fall into Spring when creating a landscape design plan. Fall into Spring will reach around 35′ x 25′ at maturity, fitting neatly into any regular-sized, full-sun greenscape.

White Oak leaves have rounded lobes and red fall color.

Ranging from Atlantic Canada southward to North Carolina, the White Oak is one of America's foundation trees. A large, hardwood tree, the impressive wide reaching branch structure holds up large leaves with rounded lobes that are distinct in the forest or open landscape. Unlike the Red Oak, leaves of White Oaks do not produce fall color; rather, they turn a russet brown and hang onto the branches until spring. Medium-sized acorns, which mature in their second year, are a favorite of squirrels and other wildlife. Sowing the acorns readily produces saplings and expansive stands of White Oak are easily established in nature or by landscapers. The bark of the White Oak is smooth and light grey during youth, but matures to a deeply furrowed texture covering a massive bole. A long-lived tree, *Quercus Alba* specimens have been dated to over 450 years. The Chestnut Oak, Overcup Oak, and the Water Oak are also members of the White Oak family, that are found growing throughout the northeastern coastal region.

In the modern landscape, the White Oak plays a vital role, along with other large trees, in helping to shade houses and lands. Shade from a tree such as the White Oak can cool a house and significantly lower air conditioning needs, saving a homeowner on their electric bills. The shade can also protect lawn space from the hot summer sun, leading to a reduced need for sprinkler system watering and enhanced personal use of lawn areas. Hardwood trees also reduce noise and air pollution in urban areas.

White Oak groves were traditionally used as natural sanctuaries for pagan groups in the first few centuries of the common era.

Historically, White Oaks groves, which grew in enormous proportions across Europe, were the sanctuaries for Pagan worship. When storms crossed the land and low electrical resistance brought lightning strikes to those groves, Pagans gathered the shattered pieces of White Oak wood to wear as amulets. The broken pieces of oak wood were seen as a symbol of survival. In the Pagan tradition, the amulets provided protection against Thor, the Germanic god of thunder.

Originally, White Oak was a Pagan symbol for the massive endurance of life across the universe, especially in the face of adversity. Later, White Oak was reinterpreted by early Christians as a representation of Jesus, and the intertwining of Pagan and Christian traditions is still evident today in the symbolism of the White Oak. Many Christians accept the White Oak's color to be a representation of the purity of Mary in the Catholic tradition and Jesus in the Protestant.

Northern Red Oak

Red Oak leaves have pointed lobes and reddish brown fall color. Other than leaf shape, the White Oak and Red Oak are similar.

The oaks are a massive botanical family, both figuratively and literally. *Quercus* family members are some of the largest and most important trees known to mankind, with Dendrologists detailing two major categories, red and white. The Red Oak is easy to recognize, with sharply pointed leaf lobes; while its cousin, the White Oak, has rounded blunt leaves. Red Oaks are generally broken into two sub-categories: the Northern Red Oak and the Southern Red Oak, with heat tolerance and density rate being the only major differences.

The state tree of New Jersey, Northern Red Oak is a long-lived, native tree in the mixed hardwood forest. Felled specimen ring counts have been recorded at over 400 years, but it is capable of living much longer. Connecticut and Rhode Island have some of the oldest Red Oak growth in America. The Northern Red Oak's native range is from southwestern Ontario east to the Atlantic Provinces of Canada and southward along the east coast to North Carolina.

Ranunculus or Persian Buttercup

A somewhat rare ornamental for the Mid-Atlantic region, Persian Buttercups flower early in the season and provide cool-weather color to the full-sun border. A rewarding perennial for patient and diligent gardeners, the Persian Buttercup can be quite fussy and hard to position. The roots of the Persian Buttercup cannot withstand frozen ground, and the flowers cannot withstand temperatures above 75 degrees Fahrenheit for extended periods. In the right spot, however, the Persian Buttercup is an outstanding flower to follow Crocus in the decorative, Spring bed.

Native to Iran, which has historically been known as Persia, the Ranunculus is sacred in the Bahá'í faith that originated in that region. In the Bahá'í faith, the arrangement and unfolding of the Persian Buttercup petals represent the orderliness that mankind should follow. The Bahá'í faith believes, like the Persian Buttercup petals, that mankind is an individual and part of a greater, universal arrangement. Therefore, Persian Buttercups are occasionally planted around the grounds of the Bahá'í gardens in Haifa, Israel. Because of its association with the Bahá'í faith, and not Islam, the Persian Buttercup is banned in its native Iran.

Rhododendron or Rhodo

An old-fashioned flowering shrub for the modern garden.

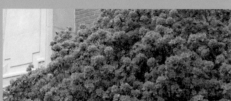

Spring flowering shrubs, Rhododendrons are one of the largest ornamentals for the northern shade garden. While thought of as a mountain shrub, Rhodos will thrive in shady coastal areas, provided they have moist, acidic soil. The Rhododendron shrub is multi-stemmed, somewhat uniform in shape and covered in large, thick, lanceolate leaves that are always matte green. They can be either evergreen or deciduous, depending on species. In early to mid-spring, Rhodos are covered in large clusters of brightly colored flowers that can last for months. Flowers can range in color from white to deep red, often with speckles near the stamens.

The Rhododendron is a member of the family Ericaceae, a vast group of angiosperms that contain many geneses and species. One of the most cosmopolitan flowering plant families, Rhododendrons can be found growing all over the world. Most botanists agree they are native to China and Japan, but there are Rhododendron species that originated in America. Gardeners in the United States generally recognize two species of Rhododendrons as being the most important for ornamental flower gardening: Azaleas in the south and Rhododendrons in the north.

In the Language of Flowers, a Victorian-era code of symbolism, Rhododendron was a symbol for passion and temperance, along with the thought of "caregiver of the unfortunate." Rhododendrons are represented in books of botanical illustrations that date to the early 1700s and are listed in some of the earliest collected texts of horticulture from Europe. In its native China, the Rhododendron is a symbol for womanhood and is ascribed feminine attributes of beauty.

Rhus Typhina
Staghorn Sumac

A native plant, Sumac attracts all manner of wildlife.

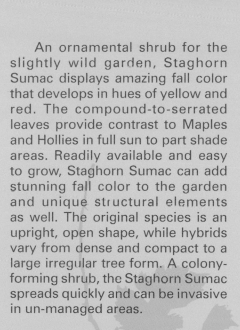

An ornamental shrub for the slightly wild garden, Staghorn Sumac displays amazing fall color that develops in hues of yellow and red. The compound-to-serrated leaves provide contrast to Maples and Hollies in full sun to part shade areas. Readily available and easy to grow, Staghorn Sumac can add stunning fall color to the garden and unique structural elements as well. The original species is an upright, open shape, while hybrids vary from dense and compact to a large irregular tree form. A colony-forming shrub, the Staghorn Sumac spreads quickly and can be invasive in un-managed areas.

R

Rose

Roses are red, and white, and pink, and orange, and yellow and bi-colored.

Gardeners have been growing Roses for centuries and they are cultivated for a range of uses around the world, including: ornamental decoration, perfume, cut flowers, beverages, medicine and municipal and cultural symbolism. Roses hybridize easily and there are hundreds of varieties in cultivation. They range in appearance from small, single-petal patterns to full peony style with a whirled petal arrangement. Roses have a color palette that spans the color wheel, with every color and variation that one can desire. The plant itself is most often an upright, multi-branched shrub with pronounced prickles, but some are trailing, scandent climbers. They are the most recognizable and esteemed flower in American, Asian, Australian, and European cultures.

According to the British film *Greenfingers* (Samuel Goldwyn films, 2001), a white Rose symbolizes purity, a red Rose symbolizes passion and a yellow Rose symbolizes the end of an affair. According to Greek mythology, Aphrodite, while hurrying to the side of dying Adonis, pushed her way through a hedgerow of white Roses and was scratched by the prickles. Therefore, the petals of the Rose are forever tainted red with her blood.

A traditional symbol of love, the classic Rose is also the state flower of New York. As featured on the front cover of Roy Heizer's book *Atlanta's Garden Plants*, the Rose is also the state flower of Georgia, in that case, a specific Rose; the Cherokee Rose.

Horse Tongue Lily or Spike in the Field

This specialty plant will add mystery
and interest to the specimen garden.

Rare in the northeastern
garden, Mouse Thorn is
worth seeking out.

Native to Europe and the Middle
East, *Ruscus Hypoglossum* is a
unique plant for the Mid-Atlantic
shade garden and quite rare in
America. What appear to be leaves
extending from the main stem
are actually not leaves at all, but
rather cladodes. A cladode is a
flattened continuation of the stem,
or more simply, a flattened modified
branch. The leaves of the *Ruscus
Hypoglossum* actually present as
a small spike-like protrusion in the
center of each cladode. This leaf
morphology is where *Ruscus* gets its
common name, Spike in the Field. A
summer flowerer, *Ruscus* blossoms
at the node or point where the leaf
grows out of the cladode. The tiny
white flower dangles like an earring
waiting to be pollinated by ants.

Spike in the Field is a close
relative of both Monkey Grass
(*Liriope*) and Solomon's Seal
(*Polygonatum*). A small evergreen
shrub that rarely tops two feet tall,
Spike in the Field compliments
Hostas and Ferns in a border.

Rue, a Citrus relative native to the Balkans, is an old-fashioned herb that is shrouded in mystery. Largely unknown to the modern gardener, Rue is an upright, semi-evergreen, flowering perennial herb. The fleshy bluish-green leaves strongly resemble Dusty Miller (*Jacobaea Maritima*) when viewed en masse, while individual leaves approximate the outline of "clubs," the card-game suit, with Rue serving as its inspiration. Rue has paniculate clusters of small, bright-yellow flowers that form in June or July and sit above 24"-tall, herbaceous stems.

Ruta Graveolens, thought of as a magical herb in the tradition of the earth religions of eastern Europe, was utilized in the defense against nefarious forces of the universe. It was an important component in spells and incantations in the years B.C.E., and was commonly available to the home gardener in the absence of a priest or priestess. While Rue's historical connections to ancient peoples are known, those associations continue to be opaque, yet intriguing.

In the Catholic tradition, priests in Italy were said to have used sprigs of Rue to sprinkle holy water on practitioners, as Rue was a symbol of regret, sorrow, and repentance. Catholic priests were also attuned to the idea that Rue was a panacea — an herbal representation of the absolution for sins.

Biblical scholars have suggested that Rue may have been used by Jews, in some parts of southeastern Europe, as maror, or bitter herb, at the Passover Seder table. The Hebrew scriptures are not specific as to which herb is to be used, and as a result local availability is considered. Rue is widely known to have a disagreeable taste, and Rue's place in the bitter herb narrative

Rue or Common Rue or Herb of Grace

is plausible. Also in the Jewish tradition, Rue's purgative effects would have coincided with the tradition of Yom Kippur. Atonement, a figurative purging of sins, is a key element in the Yom Kippur service.

More recently, historians have suggested that artists such as Leonardo da Vinci and Michelangelo sought out Rue medicinally, to enhance creativity. Several other medicinal uses, including concoctions for treating colic, coughing, and hysteria, have been noted by historians, but modern herbalists do not recommend it's use as an internal remedy, sighting allergic reactions in a high number of patients. Also, herbalists do not recommend Rue's employment as an external poultice, as it is widely known to cause severe skin irritations for some people, especially when applied during hot weather.

Salvia Ssp.
Salvia or May Night or Mainacht

The botanical name Salvia comes from the Latin word for "healing."

A garden classic, May Night or Salvia is among the most planted and reliable perennials for a sunny coastal border. A multitude of six- or seven-inch inflorescences whirl above a low growing mound of heavily textured leaves. Small, dark purple flowers bunch on the arching floral stems. This Salvia blossoms reliably in May, leading to the name May Night.

The May Night Salvia is a hybrid that originated in Germany, where it is called *Mainacht* in German. *Mai* is German for the "month of May" and *nacht* is German for "night."

A cold-hardy perennial, Mainacht can be grown with ease from gardening zones 3 to 8, making it suitable for planting over much of America and Europe. Salvias are among the most planted of all garden perennials. Originally, most Salvia's were native to central Europe and the Mediterranean region, with some varieties native to North and Central America.

An old wives' tale from France says that if one wears Salvia flowers around the neck, they will be saved from being assailed by public *pasquinades*.

The botanical name Salvia comes from the Latin word *Salvare*, which means "to save" or "to heal." Though once a wild herb, they have been in human cultivation for thousands of years. Once used for its mystic qualities by religious leaders during sacred rituals, the name "Sage" came to be used for the leader and the plant itself.

In the Islamic tradition, sweet smelling herbs are placed on Muslim graves in Palestine. Muslim scholars list Salvia as the primary herb for this practice.

Sanguinaria Canadensis
Bloodroot or Starflower

The sap of the Blood Root looks like blood. Native Americans would have appreciated this woodland perennial.

Bloodroot is a small, spring-blossoming, woodland perennial known for both its flower and its unique leaf shape. The flowers of Bloodroot are the first part of the plant to emerge in the spring, before the hardwood trees have leafed out, making the most of springtime sunlight. The radial, star-shaped, pure-white flowers that emerge low to the forest floor give the appearance of a starlit night across the heavens when seen in an open setting. The common name, Starflower, comes from this viewpoint. Starflower is a low-growing, herbaceous groundcover that never develops woody parts.

The leaves of Bloodroot, which emerge just after the flowers in late spring, are considered unique and fun by natural gardeners. The Bloodroot leaves are irregular and deeply lobed, with edges that are curved and rounded. Small and upright upon sprouting, the leaves eventually become six to nine inches across and face straight up at the tree canopy.

Bloodroot gets its most commonly used name from the bright-red sap that flows forth from a cut in the root. Historically, the blood colored sap was used by Native American tribes and frontiersmen as a clothing dye. Bloodroot dye stains and sets naturally, needing no further procedure for success. The red sap was also utilized medicinally by Native Americans for a number of ailments, but has now been deemed toxic by modern science.

Bloodroot is a distant relative of Buttercups, Columbine, Clematis, Delphiniums, and Ranunculus. It grows both wild and cultivated in its native North America, from Atlantic Canada along the east coast all the way to Florida and west to the Mississippi River. Wildlife and native plant enthusiasts appreciate the range of bees, butterflies and moths that are drawn to the flowers of the Bloodroot.

Sarcococca Confusa

Christmas Box or Sweet Box

An evergreen,
flowering shrub.

Christmas Box

A lush evergreen shrub, Christmas Box is widely planted for its fragrant white flowers that appear in mid-December. The sweet effluvium of the small stringy blossoms brings a honey Gardenia essence to the winter garden. Blossoms on the Christmas Box develop at each node along the length of the stem where the opposite leaves emerge. A shrub, the hardy upright to arching Christmas Box is in full ornamental display for the Holiday Season and through the winter months. Along with the flowers, Christmas Box produces small, shiny, black berries that attract birds in the winter.

Christmas Box is able to sustain turgidity and color for many days after cutting, and it is a common household decoration for the Christmas season. Christians appreciate the pure white fragrant flowers, and the Christmas Box has become a symbol of the purity and sweetness of the baby Jesus in the Christian tradition.

Sassafras Albidum

Sassafras or American Sassafras

An under-utilized native tree. Sassafras is sought after by wildlife and native gardeners alike for its beauty and ease of care.

As one of the most recognized American trees, Sassafras is known for its unique leaf configurations that present randomly in any of three shapes: simple, mitten (bi-lobal), and claw (tri-lobal). Few other trees have this morphology, and this identifying feature makes the Sassafras both interesting and desirable. A highly fragrant tree that produces brilliant fall color, *Sassafras Albidum* is sought by native tree enthusiasts and landscapers, who are increasingly planting it in natural areas. A medium-sized, deciduous tree or shrub with few natural pests, small white flowers, and unusual leaves, Sassafras fits well into urban or rural landscapes. The native range of Sassafras is from southern Maine to Florida and west to Missouri.

This low-growing understory plant flourishes in sun or shade and is important in the wildlife cycle. The American beaver, white tailed deer, woodchucks, and cottontails graze on its leaves and young branches in the spring and summer. The fruits of the Sassafras are eaten by several birds, including: cardinals, crested flycatchers, finches, northern mockingbirds, wild turkey, and woodpeckers.

Several varieties of forest mammals also feed on the small, dark-blue fruit. This symbiotic relationship is essential to the natural survival of both critters and Sassafras, wherein the critters are fed and the Sassafras garners seed dispersal.

In the centuries before European colonists came to America, Native Americans used the Sassafras tree for its wood and root oil. The wood supplied lumber and the oil was used as an aromatherapy as well as a therapeutic tea. During the development of the American Colonies in the 17th century, Sassafras trees were a major export chattel to England and France, where its durable wood, medicinal root, as well as ornamental qualities were appreciated. After cotton and tobacco, Sassafras trees were the largest export from America at that time.

Because the natural oils in its wood burn easily, Sassafras has been utilized as a fire starter throughout the centuries. Due to its quick natural growth, Sassafras is one of the first trees to regenerate in a forest after wildfires have decimated the tree population. Therefore, this renewable resource is prized in modern times as firewood.

Saxifraga
Saxifraga or Stonebreaker

The genus *Saxifraga* is largely unknown to American gardeners, but the family boasts more than 400 members native to the Holarctic region. Members of *Saxifraga* are short, nearly groundcover perennials that flower profusely in the spring. Saxifraga plants have small flowers borne singly, on upright wiry stems over a bed of tattered, lush-green foliage. Brightly colored flowers range from white to red. When not in flower, Saxifraga can withstand moderate foot traffic and is an excellent choice to line a garden pathway.

Saxifraga is a cold-hardy perennial, withstanding harsh winters in coastal Maine with ease. In fact, Saxifraga can be successfully grown all the way to zone 3 in central Canada. Saxifraga grows well in dry, rocky locations and growers encourage the inclusion of Stonebreaker in the Maine and New Hampshire coastal garden.

The botanical name is derived from the old Latin name *Saxum*, meaning "rock," and *frangor,* "to break" or "fracture." The common name comes from the botanical name, but is somewhat misleading. The common name Stonebreaker, in this case, does not mean stones or rocks from the earth, but rather kidney stones in the body. In ancient times this plant was thought to break stones in the bladder and kidneys.

Fan Flower or Fairy Fan Flower

Scaevola makes a wonderful hanging basket plant.

Native to coastal areas of tropical Australia and Hawaii, Fan Flower is a wonderful annual in the northeastern seaside garden. A low-mounding plant that tends to have a cascading habit, Fan Flower adds color and texture to the coastal summer border. Gardeners in urban areas that maintain container or planter box gardens in the summer months will be pleased with Fan Flower's performance. When planted in mid-May, *Scaevola* will be happily flowering purple, lavender, yellow or white by mid-June. Blossoms of the Fan Flower will produce annual color until the first hard frost in the fall. The unique fan-shaped flowers have five petals on only half the flower head, giving Fan Flower an interesting visual display. The common name Fan Flower or Fairy Fan Flower comes from the blossom's resemblance to an old fashioned, hand-held fan. This morphology is unique to the Scaevola family.

One of the *Scaevolas* common names, Fairy Fan Flower, comes from an Australian folklore story. In the tale, one hot summer day many years ago, garden fairies plucked half the petals off of a radial flower to make handheld fans for themselves. The breeze created by the many fanning fairies cooled the gardens, and the radial flower was known from then on as Fairy Fan Flower. The legend also says that any seaside garden without these flowers was doomed to fail because the fairies, unable to withstand the heat, would only populate gardens with Fairy Fan Flowers. As a result of this tale, the Fairy Fan Flowers became wildly popular throughout the seaside tropics. Legend says that this tale is the origin of what people know today as "A tropical breeze."

Climbing Hydrangea

A traditional woody vine for
fences, walls, and trellis.

Once established, Climbing Hydrangea provides years of graceful texture, shape, and flowering to the New England and Mid-Atlantic shade garden. Climbing Hydrangea is perfect for attaching to, and climbing up, brick or stone walls that edge a border. Climbing Hydrangeas, as young specimens, start out slowly when first planted, developing a thick canopy of leaves. With age, a Climbing Hydrangea Vine will wind its way to the top of a vertical wall while developing a more open, branched pattern that displays its distinctive exfoliating bark along the length of the many stems. A scandent vine, Climbing Hydrangea displays many rough looking stems that are heavily layered with peeling bark. Small roots along the stem attach themselves to bricks or rocks, keeping the vine secured on a porous and perpendicular surface.

A deciduous vine native to Japan, Climbing Hydrangea leaves emerge early in the season with a "Ragged Heart" appearance, followed shortly by a multitude of pure white mop head style flowers that are reminiscent of the Hydrangea family. The flowers light up the Climbing Hydrangea's dark shady spot with a bright clean look that compliments other shrub Hydrangeas in the shade area. In the fall, Climbing Hydrangeas flower heads develop a "dried floral arrangement" look that hangs on well into the winter. The dried flowers can easily be cut off at the end of the season and used in indoor arrangements. The leaves turn a bright clear yellow that lasts for several weeks in Delaware, Maryland, and New Jersey.

Scilla or Melancholy Bouquet

Blue, pink, or white ...the choice is yours.

A bulb perennial related to Hyacinth, Scilla is a wonderful selection for the dappled shade woodland garden. A profuse spring bloomer, the Scilla flowers emerge in dangling form along six- to eight-inch spikes above the narrow strap style foliage. The dazzling blossoms are similar in size and shape to Lily of the Valley (*Convallaria*), but flare more at the tips of the petals. A subtle stripe of color runs the length of each petal from the axis to the apex. The stripe is the same color as the rest of the petal, only a darker hue. Several color and size varieties are available to the home gardener, including: light blue, medium blue, medium blue with hints of purple, as well as pink. Scilla sizes vary from low growing to over 12". Whether displayed en masse, inter-planted among other bulbs or as a single cluster, Scilla will add a diversity of flower color and texture to the coastal garden. Left alone, Scilla will naturalize and spread throughout the area. The individual unwanted plants, however, are easy for gardeners to pull.

Silene Coronaria Syn. Lychnis
Rose Campion or Catchfly

Silene seeds were recently found in the Russian permafrost of northern Siberia. The viable seeds were grown into flowering specimens.

The botanical name for this flowering biennial is a bit confusing, with some botanists referring to it as *Lychnis* and others, *Silene*; either way it is universally referred to by its common name, Rose Campion. This old-fashioned member of the Carnation family has been planted in American gardens since the late 1700s, and in European, Middle Eastern, and Russian borders B.C.E..

The soft wool-like leaves of the Rose Campion are light grey and resemble Lamb's Ear (Stachy's), with the exception of its petiole-less morphology the tall crookedly upright stems hold aloft bright fuchsia red flowers in the summer months. The corolla of the Rose Campion is simple but complete, forming a circular configuration over the calyx. Gardeners grow Rose Campion both for the flower and the texture of the leaves. A rather un-robust flower, the Rose Campion is stunning in the dry sunny zone 5, 6 or 7 garden, but is short lived in the border and does not survive long once cut for arrangements.

As a biennial, the Rose Campion has a two year life cycle, but will self-seed in the garden, providing gardeners with years of enjoyment

for relatively little work. Gardeners who wish to keep Rose Campion need to avoid deadheading the seed pods in the fall.

Rose Campion is a close relative of Sweet William (*Dianthus*), Baby's Breath (*Gypsophila*) and *Colobanthus quitensis*, or Antarctic Pearlwort, one of only two flowering plants to survive and grow on Antarctica. With less hair, some varieties of *Silene* have green leaves and resemble a begonia leaf.

Silene Coronaria is also a close relative of *Silene Stenophylla*, an ancient white flowering Campion long thought extinct. Recently, though, *Silene Stenophylla* was regenerated from seed tissue found buried in the northeastern Siberian permafrost. The *Silene Stenophylla* discovery was made by a team of Russian scientists, who found the seeds encapsulated in ice deposits within fossil burrows that were dated at 30,000 to 32,000 years old. Once regenerated, the White Campion flowered, and produced viable seeds. The regeneration, growth and flowering of a plant from seed more than 3,000 years old is a historical first for the horticultural sciences.

Stachys Byzantina
Lamb's Ear or Woundwort

Who doesn't love Lamb's Ear? It has been a garden favorite since colonial times

One of the most widely known garden perennials, Lamb's Ear is grown for its soft, furry, grey to silver foliage and warmly colored purple flower spikes. The abundant leaves of this old-fashioned favorite are soft and velvety, developing in whirls along the sprawling and irregular stems. The shape and texture of the leaf resembles in many ways that of a baby Lamb's ear, hence the common name. A tough persistent perennial for full sun or dappled shade, Lamb's Ear adds immeasurably to the texture of a garden design plan without adversely affecting the color scheme. Lamb's Ear needs occasional cleanup to look its best, but the time and effort goes a long way in adding to the beauty of the summer garden. Lamb's Ear is closely related to the Mints, and Spearmint and Peppermint make excellent companion plants.

Although not originally native to America, Lamb's Ear naturalized here during colonial days and it is included in many historical gardens. Traditional and natural gardeners appreciate the diverse wildlife that this plant attracts to the garden. In the summer, the flowers draw several types of bees, butterflies, and moths. These insects, in turn draw birds to the garden, perpetuating the natural cycle of life for another season.

Beyond its use as an ornamental garden plant, *Stachys* has been used as a medicinal plant throughout the temperate regions of the world for centuries. Historically, herbalists have noted its usefulness in treating wounds. Ancient Romans called this plant Woundwort, and would have considered it a regular part of daily and military life. Roman Soldiers used the leaves of the Woundwort on the battlefield to act as a gauze pad replacement, while women would have used it to help apply creams and ointments. It is lost to history where the botanical name *Stachys* originated, but Byzantina, the second scientific name assigned to this plant by Carolus Linnaeus, is a reference to this plant's prominence around the Mediterranean Sea during the years of the Byzantine Empire.

Stachys Officinalis
Betony or Heal-All

Sell your coat, and eat Betony.

A close relative of Lamb's Ear and a distant relative of mint, Betony is a panacea among herbal remedies. So useful is Betony as a medicinal herb, that William Shakespeare was credited with saying "He who is of the world shall be called Betony."

Growing wild and cultivated in gardens across Europe and America, Betony has been in use for centuries. The history of its healing qualities has come down through the ages from the ancient Greeks. It has been noted in the healing of strokes and cataracts. An ancient saying from Italy states "Sell your coat and eat Betony," a reference to its ability to cure the common cold.

The Voynich Manuscript is a mysterious, as yet un-deciphered, text from the early 15th century. Although the text is in a completely unknown language, it is thought to be an herbal, as it contains many drawings of unidentified plants. The greatest botanists and herbalists in the world have so far been able to positively identify only one of the plants in *The Voynich Manuscript*, although Betony has been proposed as one of the mystery plants. *Symphytum Officinale* is also thought to be among the drawings in *The Voynich Manuscript*.

Even today, Betony is believed by some to be a charm against all manner of devil, evil, and dark visions. It can be found listed in books of spells and black magic. Due to this history, Betony's purple flowers can be found growing in both public and private gardens in Salem, Massachusetts.

There are several species of *Stachyurus* native to Asia where the species originated, but *Stachyurus Praecox* is native to Japan. The Latin name *Stachy* means spike and the suffix *urus* or *Auros* means "tail," leading to the common name Spike Tail. The second Latin name. *Praecox,* means "early," and refers to the flower time in March or April.

Stachyurus Praecox is considered sacred in the Buddhist tradition in Japan and China. The long racemes are laced together to form extended strands that are utilized as decoration in sacred spaces. The Buddhist tradition says that the fruit, a representation of life, will bring knowledge to the one who adorns with it. The strands themselves are also considered sacred, conveying the idea of the continuous stream of compassion, enlightenment, and knowledge.

Styrax Japonica

Snowbell or Japanese Snowbell

A small flowering tree native to Japan.

An upright shrub for the natural area, Snowbell brightens shady spots with its abundance of pure white flowers that dangle under the leaves along the length of arching branches. The bell-shaped flowers emerge in spring and last into summer, creating a gathering place for bees, birds, and butterflies. When viewed from a distance, the Snowbell appears to be draped in all the glory of a new-fallen snow, hence the common name Snowbell.

Later in the summer, as the flowers fade, the lush simple leaves and elongated stems of the Snowbell provide an upright structural element to the part sun coastal garden. *Styrax Japonica* can easily withstand the relatively mild winters of coastal Delaware, Maryland, New Jersey, and New York, but may die back further north.

The origin of the *Styrax* as a genus is convoluted, with species native to Europe, the Middle East, and Asia. *Styrax Japonica* is often confused with *Styrax Japonicum* and many botanists consider them the same plant. *Styrax Japonica* is most likely a relative of *Styrax Obassia*, a small tree that is native to China. All *Styrax* species are closely related to Azaleas, Blueberries, and Silverbells in the family *Ericales*.

Comfrey or Quaker Comfrey or Boneset

Comfrey, a European native cultivated since at least 450 B.C.E., has been planted in American gardens since colonial days. A beautiful flowering herb, Comfrey is useful as both a medicinal and ornamental perennial.

In the historical garden Comfrey was cultivated for use as an external poultice. High in antioxidants, it was applied to damaged muscles and broken bones during the original Olympic Games in Greece to relieve pain and speed healing of the injured athletes. The common name Boneset is derived from this practice, while the botanical name means "grown together" in Greek. In America, colonial alchemists appreciated its ability to reduce swelling around sprains or arthritic joints. Comfrey poultice was also used to treat cuts and open wounds. While its external medicinal qualities are lauded, Comfrey is known to cause organ damage and internal use is strongly discouraged.

Historically, Quakers were pacifists and objected to war on religious grounds, leading many Quaker women to become nurses. Quaker Comfrey, home-grown in the garden, was often utilized in their treatment of wounded soldiers.

Modern gardeners appreciate Comfrey as a stunning ornamental perennial with pendulous bell-shaped flowers and softly pubescent leaves that give this plant a classic garden appearance in zones 3 to 9. Comfrey performs best when grown in full sun and well-drained soil, but can stand consistently moist locations better than many perennials. The bluish purple flowers emerge on foot tall stems in mid-summer and last well into the fall, while the foliage stays fresh until the first hard frost of winter. Comfrey draws and retains many micro nutrients and it makes rich reliable compost in the coastal organic garden.

Asiatic Sweetleaf
or Sweetleaf or Sapphireberry

A medium-sized spring flowering tree for the New
England coast.

A medium-sized tree from
China, Asiatic Sweetleaf looks like
it is covered in snow when the
flowers are fully out in early May.
The puffy spherical blossoms of
the Asiatic Sweetleaf develop in
twisted panicles that droop and
sway at the tips of the branches.
The botanical name *Paniculata* is
the Latinized version of *Panicle*,
meaning the configuration of the
flowers. The brilliant white flowers
of the Sweetleaf are on display
for appreciation and pollination
over the summer, developing into
loose clusters of dark, sapphire
blue berries late in the season. The
berries remain on this tree until well
into winter, contrasting stunningly
against freshly fallen snow. The
common name Sapphireberry refers
to the rich blue berry set.

Asiatic Sweetleaf is an
outstanding ornamental tree for
the New England coastal area from
Portland, Maine to New Haven,
Connecticut. As adaptable as it is
easy to care for, Asiatic Sweetleaf
holds ornamental beauty for the
coastal garden year round. Spring
flowers, summer shade, fall berries
and winter branch structure are the
first four reasons for gardeners to
include Asiatic Sweetleaf in the year-
round landscape design plan.

Syringa
Lilac

A traditional flowering shrub, Lilacs have been a beloved plant in the northern garden for over two centuries.

An old-fashioned shrub, common Lilacs are ubiquitous across landscapes from New England south to Maryland and west to Iowa. Spring flowering traditionally brings bright bouquets of color to the ornamental garden. The original Lilacs have purple or white, while newer cultivars sometimes display bi-colored flowers and are available in regular or dwarf sizes. A cool weather shrub, Lilac flowers early in the spring before the heat of summer rises.

The Lilac flower morphology is somewhat unique in that it appears to have four petals, when, in fact, it only has one. The single petal has four defined lobes, with each lobe being curled back or cupped forward at its apex. While this morphology is not completely unique to the Lilac,

it is rare. The Lilac is an upright irregularly shaped woody deciduous shrub reaching around twenty feet in height. While the Lilac will thrive in full sun in New England, it needs some shade in the Mid-Atlantic region. Lilacs are closely related to Ash trees, Fringe trees and Privets in the Olive family, *Oleaceae*.

In the *Language of Love*, a Victorian era code of etiquette, the Lilac was said to be "The beginning of the feeling of love." The Victorian era also saw the Lilac used in mourning practices. The widow and any immediate family members were expected to wear the darkest purple or black varieties as a sign of loss. After one year of wearing a dark Lilac flower, a lighter purple could be worn.

The beauty of the Lilac flower is unrivaled in the New England landscape.

The Lilac has significance in many different religions. In the Christian tradition, purple is a royal color, the color of Christ. White Lilac flowers are also venerated in the Christian tradition, for the association of white with the purity and innocence of Jesus. Lilac flowers, which blossom in early spring, are often used for decoration at Easter, a spring time holiday in the Christian community.

In the Islamic tradition, sending flowers for a funeral is appropriate and traditional. Muslims who live in areas where Lilacs blossom often choose them, citing their beauty and tenacity. In the Muslim tradition, Lilacs are seen as comforting to the bereaved. Muslims also plant Lilacs for traditional ornamental beauty in the garden throughout the spring season.

Jews celebrate a holiday called Purim in the spring. A joyous holiday, Lilac flowers are used to decorate the Synagogue during Purim, adding bright color and a light sweet scent to the sanctuary.

In Japan, Members of the Shinto faith decorate the temple with Lilac flowers in the spring. The Shinto faith, based loosely on the concept of reincarnation, venerate the Lilac due to its perennial and long lived nature.

Tansy or Mugwort

Tansy is an herb with many medicinal qualities.

Appreciated since ancient times, Tansy is an herb with many qualities and many stories. One such story comes from the Episcopal tradition in Europe and tells of Tansy's connection with the Easter holiday. The Rectors and Bishops used to play ball with the men in their congregation and a Tansy pastry was the prize for the team that was victorious. The pastry was made from young Tansy leaves mixed with eggs and flour. This pastry was thought to assuage the hungers of the stomach after the Lenten season. It came to be the custom to eat Tansy pastries on Easter day. In time, the pastry eating custom became symbolic of the bitter herbs eaten by the Jewish community at the time of Passover. A 17th century writer noted that Tansy should be consumed in the spring as a supplement to the salt fish eaten during Lent.

Tansy also has several medicinal benefits. Medical practitioners since the 1500s have written about Tansy's ability to help reduce the swelling caused by gout. Tansy was also noted by doctors as successful in counteracting the ill effects of winter's damp and cold. Tansy remedies for nerves, hypertension, and headaches have all been recorded.

Anti-insect qualities are one of this herb's attributes.

In the late 1800s, a butcher wrote to his local newspaper to tell the people of the Tansy's use in his butcher shop. According to his letter, his daughter brought Tansy cuttings into his shop one day and laid them on the meat counter and within minutes the counter was clear of flies. The butcher then told his daughter to bring all the Tansy cuttings she could find and they filled the shop with Tansy and not a fly was to be found. Soon, customers began to comment on the clean shop and the fresh herbal flavor in the steaks. The butcher wrote that the Tansy cuttings had increased his business sevenfold. As a result of the newspaper article, the townspeople began to plant Tansy outside their doors to keep the flies out of their homes.

For the modern gardener, the Tansy herb is a wonderfully robust garden perennial. Tansy is widely known as an insect repellent and planting it in the urban ornamental garden is productive for keeping flies and other pests away. Fruit, vegetable, and natural gardeners can enjoy the benefits of Tansy's insect repellent qualities by wearing Tansy clippings on their clothing while working in the garden without permanently removing the beneficial critters. Although generally grown for its leaves, Tansy does blossom in the late summer or early fall in multiple flower heads. Flowers of the Tansy are a bright clean yellow, and make an excellent dried flower.

Taxus or Yew

An evergreen shrub that can be sheared to a number of shapes, where it is used as a structural element.

Historically and culturally significant, Yews can today be seen planted all over the northeastern coastal region and across the American Midwest. But, the history of the Yew starts many centuries earlier in Europe.

An extremely long-lived tree, the oldest known Yew in the world is the Fortingall Yew in Perthshire, Scotland, with an estimated age of over 2000 years. The Fortingall Yew is considered an ancient specimen and the oldest tree in Europe, along with several other Yews throughout Europe that are estimated to be over 1500 years.

The genus, *Taxus*, is much older than any single living specimen and Yew artifacts have been discovered that date well over 3200 years. Recently, in Essex, England, a Yew spear found in an ancient tomb was cataloged at approximately 2900 years. Several Yew longbows have also been estimated at over 1000 years, and the Yew longbow tradition is well recorded in military history.

A professor at the University of Uppsala in the mid-1700s, botanist and father of the binomial system of nomenclature, Carlos Linnaeus, would most likely have known of The Sacred Tree of the Temple of Uppsala, located in Uppsala, Sweden. The temple was one of several sites in Europe where Yew trees were historically planted in reverence by old world Pagans. The subject of much veneration in the Pagan tradition, Yew trees symbolized longevity and life, due to their slow growing nature and evergreen foliage. The toxic red berries of the Yew are also noted in the pagan tradition, a symbol of the blood of the enemy. Even today, Yews are often planted in the landscape for the bright red berries that attract several kinds of birds. Birds are immune to the toxic substance in Yew berries, and they are the prime natural spreader of Yews. (Author's note: As a little boy, I was taken to the emergency room to get my stomach pumped

Taxus is a tough, durable, prunable, shrub with poisonous berries.

after eating the berries of a Yew shrub in my grandmother's yard in Richmond, Virginia. I learned early on that the berries are beautiful, but toxic to humans.)

Early botanical writers, such as the Greek scientist Theophrastus and the Roman naturalist Pliny the Elder describe various aspects of the Yew plant in their writings. The Yew, a frequent subject in literature, is mentioned in many poems and books, such as *Beowulf* and Arthur Conan Doyle's *Hound of the Baskervilles*. Yews are written about in works by J. R. R. Tolkien, William Wordsworth, and Anna Lewington. University of Georgia horticulture professor and author Michael Dirr relates facts about several varieties of Taxus in his works. A Yew branch wand is wielded by an evil fictional wizard in a popular English book series.

For the professional or home landscaper in the north and mid-south, Yews are a staple planting. Hardy, adaptable, and evergreen, Yews are both beautiful and versatile

in the modern greenscape. One of the Yews' best attributes for modern usage is its ability to be sheared and shaped for structural positioning in the landscape. Stout and thick, Yews accept harsh pruning over many years with a survivability rate rivaled by few other landscape shrubs. Left un-pruned, Yew shrubs will develop an open irregular branching pattern with quirky shapes. Over time, the exfoliating bark of the Yew develops magnificent desultory reddish-colored plates with each year's growth.

Yews will attract several types of wildlife to the garden, including: birds, squirrels, and insects that utilize its sturdy branches as a habitat. Since the flowers are insignificant, this shrub is most widely planted as a sculptural specimen or tall solid hedgerow barrier for sun or shade.

Thermopsis Lanceolata

False Lupine or Banner

An upright perennial in the coastal garden, False Lupine is a colorful structural choice for the sunny border. The False Lupine has a spectacular early to mid-spring inflorescence, with Banner illuminating the garden with its large, motley-colored, lupine-style flower spikes. Banner tends to colonize in the garden and may, in future years, need to be divided. Like Fish Mint or Dittany, this Asian native is long-lived, but may take a few years to reach full maturity. Gardeners need to plant Banner in enriched garden soil and water sparingly.

Thuja or Arborvitae

Medicinal and screening qualities best define the Thuja.

A member of the Cypress family, Thujas are a commonly planted evergreen shrub or tree along the northern east coast. Landscapers have several types to choose from, including large rounded shrubs and slender upright tree forms. The traditional all green variety, as well as variegated types, are available to the modern gardener. The Thuja is native from Manitoba, Canada, and grows along the east coast to Maryland, but is rarely found in the wild.

Arborvitae can be planted as a single specimen or in groupings for greater effect. Thujas are grown for their evergreen foliage, texture, and shape. The flower of the Thuja is considered insignificant by landscapers, who plant Arborvitae in the border for structural reasons.

It is known to attract deer, who eat its young leaves and can strip an entire tree in one night. The Thuja is also known to sometimes grow well for several years and then die suddenly for no explainable reason. The Thuja, upon maturity, can provide years of landscaping beauty. While screening unsightly objects, evergreen trees like the Thuja also reduce noise and air pollution in urban areas, leading to more comfortable living conditions.

The Arborvitae, Latin for "Tree of Life," is sacred in several Native American traditions. The wood of the Arborvitae is aromatic and is, in Native American culture, thought to attract the spirits of the dead to the living when it is used in séance- type rituals.

Tiarella
Foamflower

A popular native garden plant.

Foamflower is a woodland perennial for all seasons with its enchanting flowers lighting up even the deep shade border. The lobed leaves of the Foamflower display in a wide assortment of shapes and color patterns. The *Tiarella* forms healthy whirled clumps that look great all season. Landscapers use them en masse at the front of borders as edgings or specimens, or plant them in groups as groundcovers in lightly or heavily shaded natural gardens. Foamflowers prefer a rich compost mixture, but are an easy to grow evergreen in any situation except standing water.

Native to the woodlands of North America, Foamflowers are small plants with lightly pubescent serrated leaves that form mounds and spread by runners to make patches. In spring, Foamflowers display thin upright spikes of small pure white or light pink flowers. The spring blossoming flowers of the *Tiarella* are bell shaped, loosely clustered at the end of the inflorescence and usually point downward. The flower configuration is where the name Foam comes from, as the flowers are said to have a "foamy" appearance. Foamflowers, found growing wild and cultivated from New Brunswick, Canada south along the east coast to North Carolina, are an excellent native groundcover for the shade area. It develops a dense thicket of foliage that is often highlighted with attractive burgundy splotches.

Trifolium Pratense
Red Clover

Native to Europe and Asia, *Trifolium Pratense* has been naturalized in many other parts of the world, including most of North America. In America, Red Clover is considered a semi-invasive perennial wildflower. Despite its aggressiveness, the Red Clovers beauty and ability to attract wildlife convinces most urban gardeners to plant or allow it. Large populations occur naturally throughout the Mid-Atlantic region northward into New England.

While gardeners appreciate Red Clover as an ornamental wildflower, farmers rely on Red clover as horse and cattle fodder. Red Clover is a nitrogen fixer, and helps to maintain nutrient balances in soil, which in turn makes more nutritious field grazing plants. Red Clover is a Legume family member and is closely related to several important agricultural crops, including beans, peas and peanuts. It is also related to Licorice and Kudzu.

Red Clover is the state flower of Vermont, as set forth by the state assembly in 1894. The Vermont assembly chose the Red Clover for its importance to the dairy cattle industry, a major source of economic development.

A national floral emblem in Denmark, Red Clover is recognized as historically or culturally significant in that country. The Genus name, *Trifolium Pratense*, comes from the Latin for "three leaves," while *Pratense* is Latin for "of the fields." In Ireland, Clover has historically been associated with the Christian tradition for its three- or *tri-* leafed morphology. Christian tradition says that the *Trifolium* represents the Trinity.

Trillium or Birthroot

Trilliums, a wildflower, spread easily but are short lived each individual season.

An early blossoming ephemeral perennial, Trillium opens, flowers and shuts down to its roots very quickly in the spring. The flowering cycle of the Trillium lasts for only a few weeks, disappearing from the natural landscape by late April or early May. A prolific woodland plant that thrives in mixed hardwood forest areas both near the coast and further inland, Trillium can be enjoyed by nature enthusiasts from North Carolina all the way to Maine. The variegated form is known as Sweet Betsy.

The Trillium is widely recognized for its upright tri-bracted configuration and central upright flower. What appear to be three leaves are actually bracts, or flower petals that mimic leaves. The true leaves of the Trillium are underground, where this plant spends the vast majority of time.

Trillium flowers vary widely, but all of them are beautiful.

Tsuga Canadensis
Hemlock or Canadian Hemlock

A large pyramidal evergreen, the Hemlock is the state tree of Pennsylvania, with a growth range from Atlantic Canada, throughout New England and down the spine of the Appalachian mountains. The graceful swooping branches and the short, slightly whirled needles give the Hemlock a majestic and unique look that is often its main ID feature. The branches are not densely displayed, but rather open, with upturned tips. The cones of this Pine relative are small, vaguely Acorn shaped and somewhat flaky in texture. Hemlocks are noted for their ability to withstand shady forest conditions better than most conifers.

While American gardeners often think of species being imported to these shores, occasionally species that are native to America are introduced elsewhere in the world. This was the case, when, in 1736, the Canadian Hemlock was introduced to British gardens. It has thrived in England, Scotland, and other parts of northern Europe since the early 1700s.

The history of the Hemlock in folk tradition most likely started with its inclusion in a colonial diary found in Maine that dated from the 1660s. While no exact name was given in the writing, the description of this tree and its ability to withstand great amounts of snowpack on its branches without breaking lead Ethnobotanists to conclude the mentioned tree to be the Canadian Hemlock. Several references to the Canadian Hemlock have appeared in literature that predates the American Revolution.

The common name Hemlock is derived from the odor of the needles when crushed, resembling that of the unrelated poison Hemlock (*Conium Maculatum*). The leaves or needles of the *Tsuga Canandensis* are actually very high in Vitamin C, and are sometimes used as a survival food for those lost in the forest. Modern campers have noted that *Tsuga* branches are strong, yet flexible, and are useful for tent structures.

Tulips are now grown all over the world.

Tulipa
Tulip

A wildly popular garden flower, historically associated with the Netherlands.

New cultivar introductions have greatly expanded the Tulips spectrum in recent years.

While Tulips are cultivated worldwide, their cultivation is most closely associated with the Netherlands in Northern Europe. The cultivation of Tulips in the Netherlands is so traditional that it has become a part of their culture, and is referenced in everything from television to historical paintings by American artists, such as George Hitchcock.

The Netherlands and neighboring Belgium are the world's largest producers of Tulip bulbs for foreign export. For a number of years in Europe, the Tulip bulb was considered so exotic that it was used for currency, and Tulips were the basis of the Dutch economy. One could literally make a land or house payment in Tulip bulbs. When the Tulip market changed, the entire economy of northern Europe collapsed.

While many gardeners may think Tulips are native to the Netherlands, they are actually native to Southern Europe, Northern Africa, and parts of the Middle East.

Valeriana Officinalis

Valerian or Setwale or Garden Valerian

Native Americans utilized Valerian Root as a sleep aid.

Valeria is often grown alongside Tansy in the herb garden.

An old-fashioned herbal, *Valeriana Officinalis* has been cultivated in its native range, Canada southward along the east coast to Maryland, for centuries. Native Americans, the first peoples to utilize the Valerian root as a sleep aid, shared it with the earliest English colonists who quickly adopted it. While it can be grown as an ornamental garden perennial, Valerian is most widely harvested for its medicinal qualities. The root of the Valerian is known in folk and herbal remedies as a sedative, muscle relaxant, and anti-anxiety treatment.

Though it produces white or light pink flowers in small clusters on two- or three-feet tall inflorescences, the Valerian's most distinguishable ID feature is its heavily serrated bi-pinnately compound leaves and strong veining. A prolific self-seeder, *Valeriana Officinalis* is a tall growing, full sun perennial that prefers dry, nutrient rich soil.

Valerian is a close relative of Jupiter's Beard (*Centranthus Ruber*) and Seablushes (Plectritis). Companion plants for contrast and compliment include Golden Lace (*Patrinia Scabiosifolia*) and Globe Thistle (*Echinops*).

In modern pop culture, Valerian is mentioned in the 1999, Twentieth Century Fox film, *Fight Club*, where a doctor suggests to an insomniac, "Chew some Valerian root and get more exercise." Setwale, as it is called in England, is also an integral part of the plot for the episode "A Worm in the Bud," in the British detective series *Midsomer Murders* (ITV).

Vinca Major

Vinca or Periwinkle

A prolific and much loved flowering, evergreen, ground cover, Vinca is said to conceal garden fairies and gnomes from view.

A wonderful groundcover vine for most of the mid-Atlantic region, *Vinca Major* is a sprawling, spring flowering evergreen. Single blue to purple fan-shaped flowers grace the fast growing stems, while opposite glossy green leaves create an unmistakable blanket in the part sun garden. The large flowers present in mid spring and last the summer months, with the bright distinctive foliage lasting year round. Periwinkle can be cultivated as a groundcover for the landscape, but often grows wild in unmanaged forests, where its leaf canopy provides cover for all manner of insects, snakes, and other wildlife. The dense mat-like foliage that roots as it spreads, also cools the ground and helps retain groundwater.

Chaucer, an English writer and alchemist, lists its presence in England as far back as the Middle Ages. It has grown in the British Isles for hundreds of years, leading many to erroneously assume it is native to England. Periwinkle is in fact native to the continent of Europe, where Pliny the Elder, in the first century, mentions its cultivation in Rome.

A fun garden saying reminds gardeners that there is also a *V. Minor* that looks similar to *V. Major*.

Vinca big, Vinca Major is not to be confused with Vinca Minor; the differences are small, but the mistake quite major.

The flowers and the leaves of *Vinca Minor* are smaller than those of *Vinca Major*. Otherwise, these two *Apocynaceae* relatives are indistinguishable.

No less a botanical authority than Thomas Jefferson planted Periwinkle in his gardens at Monticello and Poplar Grove, in the 1780s. Periwinkle would have been widely planted among the early American colonists.

Xanthoceras Sorbifolium
Yellowhorn or Goldenhorn

A mind-blowingly stunning flowering tree.

Goldenhorn is rare in the New England landscape, but is worth finding. It makes an outstanding specimen in the upscale garden design.

Native to northern China, Goldenhorn is a medium-sized spring flowering tree. It is related to Red Maples, growing well under similar conditions, although not as far south. Goldenhorns, however, are about half the size of a mature Maple, making it an excellent choice for use as a suburban ornamental specimen. A somewhat unique tree in the New England coastal area, gardeners and landscapers are quickly discovering the Goldenhorns outstanding ornamental attributes and ease of care.

The flowers of the Goldenhorn are borne in May at the branch nodes, giving an elongated cluster display. The flower petal color is yellow or golden at the center, somewhat horn shaped with five distinct lobes that curl backward. Occasionally, the petals are stripped in red, giving the Goldenhorn flower a brush painted appearance. This tree gets its common name, Goldenhorn, from the color of its leaves and shape of its flower. An extended spring floral display adds to the desirability of Goldenhorn as an ornamental specimen. The flowers of the Goldenhorn are subtly scented, attracting bees, birds, and butterflies.

The pinnate, finely serrated leaves, too, add textural interest to the northern summer border. Upon emerging, the leaves of the Goldenhorn are a clear gold or yellow color, leading to the common name Goldenhorn or Yellowhorn. This tree gets its second botanical name, *Sorbifolium*, due to the leaves' similarities to the unrelated Sorbus Shrub. The fruit is a small, brownish pod that dangles under the branches throughout the fall season.

BIBLIOGRAPHY

Mickey, Thomas J., and Alison Beck. 2006. *Best Garden plants for New England.* Auburn, WA: Lone Pine Publishing.

Griffith, Lawrence D. 2008. *Flowers and Herbs of Early America.* Williamsburg, VA: The Colonial Williamsburg Foundation in association with Yale University Press.

Colonial Dames of America. 1995, 1970. *Herbs and Herb Lore of Colonial America*; originally published as *Simples, Superstitions & Solace: Plant material used in colonial living.* Dover Publications, Inc. and Grounds committee of the National Society of the Colonial Dames of America in the State of Connecticut.

INDEX OF COMMON PLANT NAMES

Common Name - *Botanical Name* (season)

Common Name - *Botanical Name* (season)

Cabbage - *Brassica Oleracea* (Spring), 23

California Lilac - *Ceanothus Ssp.* (Spring/Summer), 32

Candytuft - *Iberis Sempervirens* (Evergreen), 72

Canterbury Bells - *Campanula* (Summer), 26

Catalpa - *Catalpa Bignonioides* (Spring/Summer), 31

Chinese Pistache - *Pistacia Chinensis* (Summer/Fall), 106

Christmas Box - *Sarcococca confusa* (Evergreen), 121

Cigarette Plant - *Cuphea* (Spring/Summer), 47

Cinnamon Fern - *Osmunda Cinnamomea* (Summer), 94

Climbing Hydrangea - *Schizophragma Hydrangeoides* (Year Round), 125

Clubmoss - *Lycopodiaceae Ssp.* (Evergreen), 84

Coast Leucothoe - *Leucothoe Axillaris* (Spring/Summer), 81

Cockscomb - *Celosia* (Summer Annual), 34

Common Name - *Botanical Name* (season)

Fall into Spring - *Poliothyrsis Sinensis* (Spring/Summer/Fall), 109

False Lupine - *Thermopsis Lanceolata* (Summer), 140

Fescue - *Festuca* (Evergreen), 60

Firecracker Flower - *Crossandra Infundibuliformis* (Summer), 47

Flowering Quince - *Chaenomeles* (Spring/Summer), 36

Foamflower - *Tiarella* (Spring/Summer), 142

Forsythia - *Forsythia x Intermedia* (Spring/Summer), 61

Ghost Tree - *Davidia Involucrata* (Year Round), 50

Golden Seal - *Hydrastis Canadensis* (Spring/Summer), 71

Golden Star - *Chrysogonum* (Spring/Summer), 40

Goldenhorn - *Xanthoceras Sorbifolium* (Spring/Summer), 149

Greater Celandine - *Chelidonium Majus* (Spring), 37

Ground Orchid - *Bletilla Striata* (Spring/Summer), 20

Common Name - *Botanical Name* (season)

Hardy Rubber Tree - *Eucommia Ulmoides* (Spring/Summer/Fall), 55

Hawthorn - *Crataegus* (Spring/Summer), 44

Heart's a Bustin'- *Euonymus Americana* (Spring/Summer/Fall), 57

Hemlock - *Tsuga Canadensis* (Evergreen), 145

Honesty - *Lunaria Annua* (Spring/Summer Biennial), 82

Hops - *Humulus Lupulus* (Spring/Summer/Fall), 69

Hornbeam - *Carpinus Caroliniana* (Summer), 30

Hosta – *Hosta* (Spring/Summer), 68

Jerusalem Sage - *Phlomis Fruticosa* (Spring/Summer), 101

Kentucky Coffee Tree - *Gymnocladus Dioicus* (Spring/Summer), 66

Knotweed - *Fallopia Japonica* (Spring/Summer), 59

Kolomikta Kiwi - *Actinidia Kolomikta* (Spring/Summer/Fall), 11

Lamb's Ear - *Stachys Byzantina* (Spring/Summer/Fall), 128

Common Name - *Botanical Name* (season)

Common Name - *Botanical Name* (season)

Peony - *Paeoniaceae* (Spring/Summer), 95

Periwinkle - *Vinca Major* (Spring/Summer), 148

Persian Buttercup - *Ranunculus* (Spring/Summer), 113

Pussytoes - *Antennaria* (Summer), 12

Red Clover - *Trifolium Pratense* (Spring/Summer), 143

Red Oak - *Quercus Rubra* (Year Round), 112

Rhododendron - *Rhododendron* (Spring/Summer), 114

Rose - *Rosa* (Spring/Summer), 116

Rose Campion - *Silene Coronaria* (Spring/Summer), 127

Rue - *Ruta* (Evergreen), 118

Russian Sage - *Perovskia Atriplicifolia* (Spring/Summer/Fall), 99

Salvia - *Salvia* (Spring/Summer/Fall), 119

Sassafras - *Sassafras Albidum* (Spring/Summer/Fall), 122

Common Name - *Botanical Name* (season)

Common Name - *Botanical Name* (season)